RESEARCH FOUNDATION
CONTRIBUTION FORM

☑ **Yes,** I want the Research Foundation to continue to fund innovative research that advances the investment management profession. Please accept my tax-deductible contribution at the following level:

☐ Contributing Research Fellow ....$25,000 to $49,999
☐ Research Fellow ....$10,000 to $24,999
☐ Contributing Donor ....$1,000 to $9,999
☐ Donor ....$100 to $999
☐ Friend ....$ _____

☐ My check is enclosed (payable to the Research Foundation of CFA Institute).
☐ I would like to donate appreciated securities (send me information).
☐ Please charge my donation of $ _____ to my credit card.
  ☐ VISA ☐ MC ☐ Amex ☐ Diners ☐ Corporate ☐ Personal

Card Number

____ / ____
Expiration Date   Name on card PLEASE PRINT
☐ Corporate Card
☐ Personal Card
                                Signature

☐ This is a pledge. Please bill me for my donation of $_____.

☐ I would like recognition of my donation to be:
  ☐ Individual donation ☐ Corporate donation ☐ Different individual

PLEASE PRINT NAME OR COMPANY NAME AS YOU WOULD LIKE IT TO APPEAR

PLEASE PRINT ☐ Mr. ☐ Mrs. ☐ Ms.   MEMBER NUMBER _____

Last Name (Family Name)   First   Middle Initial

Title

Address

City   State/Province   Country ZIP/Postal Code
                                              4FRA

Please mail this completed form with your contribution to:
Research Foundation • P.O. Box 3668
Charlottesville, VA 22903-0668 USA

For more on the Research Foundation of CFA Institute, please visit www.cfainstitute.org and select the Research Foundation under "Featured Areas".

Tell Us
Your Research Needs

OF CFA INSTITUTE

The Research Foundation's mission is to encourage education for investment practitioners worldwide and to fund, publish, and distribute relevant research. The Foundation emphasizes research of practical value to investment professionals while exploring new and challenging topics that provide a unique perspective in the rapidly evolving profession of investment management.

These are just a few of the topics under consideration by the Research Foundation Review Board:

- ☐ Global sectors
- ☐ Risk management
- ☐ Asset allocation
- ☐ Asset and liability management
- ☐ Volatility
- ☐ Hedge funds

Please check which of these research topics you would like to see, or suggest your own topics below. Our goal is to provide research that helps you to perform your investment management duties better and to maintain your competitive edge while ultimately better serving your clients. We will offer your thoughts at an upcoming meeting of the Research Committee.

TOPIC _____

TOPIC _____

TOPIC _____

We thank you for your ideas.

Visit www.cfapubs.org for the latest investment research.

Jennifer Francis
Qi Chen
Richard H. Willis
Fuqua School of Business,
Duke University

Donna R. Philbrick
Portland State University

Security Analyst Independence

Editorial Staff
Elizabeth Collins
Book Editor

Sophia E. Battaglia
Assistant Editor

Kara H. Morris
Production Manager

Lois A. Carrier/Jesse Kochis
Composition and Production

Mission

The Research Foundation's mission is to encourage education for investment practitioners worldwide and to fund, publish, and distribute relevant research.

Biographies

Jennifer Francis is professor of accounting at the Fuqua School of Business at Duke University. Previously, she was an associate professor at the Graduate School of Business at the University of Chicago. Professor Francis's research focuses on the equity valuation implications of financial information. Her work has appeared in various journals, including the *Journal of Accounting and Economics* and the *Accounting Review*, and she serves on the editorial review boards of the *Journal of Accounting and Economics*, *Journal of Accounting Research*, and *Accounting Review*. Professor Francis is the recipient of numerous awards for outstanding teaching, including the Bank of America Outstanding Faculty Award and the Daimler-Chrysler Award for Innovation and Excellence in Teaching. She is a certified public accountant and holds a BS from Bucknell University and an MS and a PhD from Cornell University.

Qi Chen is associate professor of accounting at the Fuqua School of Business at Duke University. His research focuses on understanding the interaction between a company's accounting system and other control mechanisms in providing incentives to agents in the organization. Professor Chen's work has appeared in numerous journals, including the *Journal of Accounting Research* and *Journal of Accounting and Economics*. He holds a BA from Wuhan University, an MA from the University of Maryland at College Park, and an MBA and a PhD from the Graduate School of Business at the University of Chicago.

Donna R. Philbrick is professor of accounting at Portland State University. She also serves on the faculty of the University of Oregon Executive MBA Program. Previously, Professor Philbrick taught at Duke University. Her research, which focuses on capital market consequences of accounting disclosures, has appeared in such journals as the *Accounting Review*, the *Journal of Accounting Research*, and the *Journal of Accounting and Economics*, and she serves as an associate editor of *Accounting Horizons*. Professor Philbrick is a certified public accountant and holds a BS from the University of Oregon and an MBA and a PhD from Cornell University.

Richard H. Willis is associate professor of accounting at the Fuqua School of Business at Duke University. His research focuses on buy-side and sell-side security analysts, with an emphasis on their earnings forecasts and stock recommendations. Professor Willis's work has appeared in numerous journals, including the *Journal of Accounting and Economics* and *Journal of Accounting Research*. He is the recipient of the Daimler-Chrysler Award for Outstanding Teaching of an Elective Course and the Excellence in Teaching Award from the MBA–Cross Continent Program at Duke University. Professor Willis is a certified public accountant and holds a BS from the University of South Alabama, an MS from Ohio State University, an MBA from the Fuqua School of Business at Duke University, and a PhD from the Graduate School of Business at the University of Chicago.

Contents

Foreword vi

Preface viii

Chapter 1.   Security Analysts' Forecasting Behavior 1

Chapter 2.   Explanations of Forecast Optimism 32

Chapter 3.   Analyst Independence from
             Corporate Management 52

Chapter 4.   Analyst Independence from Other Analysts 75

Chapter 5.   Conclusion 91

References 95

Foreword

Investors have long suspected that sell-side security analysts—at least historically—have not acted independently of their employers' interests. This suspicion gained considerable credence when in April of 2003, 10 of the largest investment banks agreed to pay out more than $1.4 billion in fines, penalties, and other payments and to institute a series of reforms to settle government claims against them. The perception by most investors that analysts do not act independently derives mainly, however, from anecdotal information and media coverage of several high-profile cases of alleged abuse. What is needed is a scientific exploration of the evidence—the nature and causes of security analyst conflicts—and the potential remedies for the conflicts. Thus, we are most fortunate that Jennifer Francis, Qi Chen, Donna R. Philbrick, and Richard H. Willis have undertaken just such a study.

The authors begin by isolating the key issues, describing their data, and defining the variables they use to address various aspects of analyst independence. Specifically, they investigate the conventional view that analysts are optimistic in their forecasts of earnings by an examination of such properties as bias, accuracy, dispersion, and newsworthiness. They then seek to determine the extent to which this optimism is associated with incentives, self-selection, and cognitive biases. They find evidence of all three causes. Potential revenues from investment banking, underwriting, and (especially) brokerage trading volume lead analysts to produce unduly optimistic forecasts. Analysts also tilt their coverage toward companies with better earnings prospects. And they underreact to earnings-related information. The good news, albeit tentative, is that the intensity of these effects appears to be diminishing—perhaps because of public and regulatory scrutiny.

The authors next examine the "management relations" theory, which holds that corporate managers possess valuable information that necessitates close communication with analysts, which benefits both the company and the analysts. This theory is particularly interesting in light of the recently enacted Regulation Fair Disclosure, which curtails private communications between company managers and analysts. Anecdotal evidence suggests that analysts are subject to retribution from management if they fail to report favorably; reprisals include exclusion from meetings, outings, and conference calls. The empirical evidence is inconclusive. Yes, analysts do issue more optimistic forecasts when the incentives to curry favor with management are great, but *direct* tests of analyst reliance on company managers for information and of the effect on such reliance have so far not been possible.

The authors also explore the extent to which analysts behave independently of other analysts. Evidence of "herding" behavior in the investment industry is widespread. This behavior is attributed to fear of sanctions for deviating from the norm, payoff externalities (such as financial benefits that may arise when others follow in your tracks), and career concerns. The evidence suggests that security analysts do exhibit herding behavior in their stock recommendations and their earnings forecasts.

Francis, Chen, Philbrick, and Willis have written a comprehensive and insightful analysis of security analyst independence that should help investors evaluate the integrity of sell-side research and help regulators adopt wise policies. The Research Foundation is extremely pleased to present *Security Analyst Independence*.

Mark Kritzman, CFA
Research Director
The Research Foundation of
CFA Institute

Preface

The corporate scandals of recent years have resulted in increased scrutiny of security analysts and significant repercussions to and reforms in the investment banking industry. In particular, in April 2003, 10 of the largest investment banks agreed to pay out approximately $1.4 billion—$487.5 million in fines and penalties, $387.5 million in disgorgement of profits, $432.5 million to fund independent research, and $80 million for investor education. They also agreed to implement several reforms, including (but not limited to) prohibiting analysts from receiving compensation for investment banking activities, prohibiting analysts from being involved in the solicitation of investment banking business, and disclosure of analysts' forecasting and stock-picking ability.[1] In part as a response to concerns about untruthful reporting, the U.S. Congress passed Regulation Analyst Certification (Reg AC) effective 14 April 2003.[2] Reg AC requires analysts to certify in their reports that their expressed views accurately reflect their beliefs about the future performance of a covered company.

For years leading up to these reforms, regulators, investors, politicians, and academic researchers had suggested that analysts' relationships with company management, analysts' compensation contracts, and the pressures on sell-side analysts employed by investment banking houses contribute to a lack of analyst independence. These conflicts of interest allegedly have resulted in distortions in analysts' forecasts of earnings and target prices and in reluctance on the part of analysts to issue sell recommendations.

Much of the research examining biases in analysts' forecasts has focused on their earnings per share forecasts because such forecasts are regularly provided by most analysts and are easily benchmarked against actual earnings. The calibration against actual earnings produces a forecast error that tells the researcher whether the analyst's forecast was above or below actual earnings and by how much. Research has interpreted various aspects of the distribution of analysts' earnings forecast errors as indicators of the quality of analysts' forecasts. In particular, forecast accuracy has been assessed by using unsigned forecast errors, and signed forecast errors have been used to assess bias in analysts' forecasts. Chapter 1 describes the measurement of these variables in detail and provides descriptive evidence about them garnered over the past 23 years.

[1] For example, brokerage houses must now disclose what percentage of all their ratings are buy, hold, and sell and must clearly define the rating system they use (Financial Times.com, 15 May 2003).

[2] The final rule is available at www.sec.gov/rules/final/33-8193.htm.

Forecast errors have also been used in research into whether analysts appropriately incorporate information contained in prior realizations of economic variables, such as prior-period forecast errors, prior-period excess returns, and prior-period earnings or earnings changes. For the most part, this research has found that analysts' forecasts do not respond enough (i.e., as much as one would expect if analysts are rationally processing new information) to prior news. That is, analysts appear to underreact to recent news, with most of the underreaction evidenced by analysts' failure to revise their forecasts downward proportionately following the arrival of bad news that has implications for future earnings. [3] This underreaction creates an inefficiency in the market that is one of the explanations for the systematic bias in analysts' forecasts.

Of particular interest in understanding issues associated with analyst independence is the research related to analysts' forecast bias, accuracy, dispersion, and newsworthiness. Research in each of these areas has generally produced conflicting results. For example, research has generally reported negative *mean* forecast errors (where forecast error was computed as actual earnings minus forecasted earnings) and interpreted these negative errors as evidence of optimistic bias on the part of analysts. Conflicting results have been found with respect to the sign of *median* forecast errors, however, which have variously been reported to be positive, negative, or zero. Although not conclusive, the finding of analyst optimism has gained fairly wide acceptance among researchers, analysts, and the markets.

Researchers have also investigated factors contributing to a bias toward optimistic forecasting, including institutional incentives (such as those created by investment banking, underwriting, and the brokerage's revenue-generating functions), incentives to curry favor with client companies, self-selection (which holds that analysts prefer to follow companies about which they hold favorable views), and cognitive biases (such as those that are associated with the general underreaction phenomenon). We review this research and present new evidence on these factors in Chapters 2 and 3.

Not all researchers accept the cognitive and incentive theories that have been put forth to explain the existence of forecast optimism. Recent work (e.g., Abarbanell and Lehavy 2002, 2003; Bradshaw and Sloan 2002) suggests that the observed optimism in analysts' forecasts (and the apparent inefficiency of analysts' forecasts) may be attributable, at least in part, to data and specification issues. We review this research in Chapter 1 to provide the reader with a balanced view.

---

[3] Analysts are not the only market participants who underreact to new information. Even more severe levels of underreaction have been documented for investors.

Throughout this monograph, we confine our discussions and investigations to the forecasting behavior of sell-side security analysts.[4] Sell-side analysts are employed at brokerage houses (e.g., Merrill Lynch & Co.) and make investment recommendations to individual and/or institutional investors. Buy-side security analysts are employed by money management firms or investment firms (e.g., Fidelity Investments) and make investment decisions on behalf of clients and/or holders of mutual funds. We restrict our attention to the forecast behavior of sell-side analysts because, for the most part, the forecast data that researchers have examined is limited to forecasts provided by sell-side analysts (an exception is Willis 2001).

We also focus our discussion on research that investigated companies domiciled principally in the United States. In part because of data limitations, studies of non-U.S. companies are rare. Moreover, U.S. companies and exchanges account for the vast majority of global equity trading. In 2003, an estimated 3.1 *billion* shares changed hands daily on the New York Stock Exchange, American Stock Exchange, and NASDAQ; the daily average trading volume on exchanges in 55 non-U.S. countries with active equity markets was only 134.1 *million* shares. Not surprisingly, substantial resources are dedicated to research involving U.S. stock—an estimated $1.7 billion in 2003 for the eight largest research departments on Wall Street (Davis 2004).[5] This amount represents less than 0.01 percent, however, of the market capitalization of U.S. traded companies.

Our objective in this monograph is to review and synthesize research on analysts' forecasting behavior, particularly as that behavior relates to questions of analyst independence. Because the literature on issues related to security analyst independence is large and diverse, our summaries are by no means exhaustive. In selecting among this broad and deep body of work, we focused on articles and approaches that we viewed as making important advances in the research, documenting robust findings, or identifying controversial questions. We have tried to carefully distinguish between instances when the body of work produced consistent findings from instances when the research produced mixed or inconsistent results. In the case of consistent findings, we highlight the broad conclusions that have been drawn; in the case of inconsistent or contradictory findings, we provide our own views on how to

---

[4]For additional discussion of the environment in which sell-side security analysts work, see Asquith, Mikhail, and Au (forthcoming 2004), Eccles and Crane (1988), and Liaw (1999); for discussion of buy-side analysts and forecast bias, see Cianci (2000) and Willis (2001).

[5]The eight largest research departments (according to Davis) are at Merrill Lynch, Credit Suisse First Boston, Smith Barney, Morgan Stanley, JPMorgan Chase, Goldman Sachs, Lehman Brothers, and Bear, Stearns & Co.

interpret the evidence. In some cases, we also present the results of recent research attempting to resolve concerns with prior work to obtain more robust results or more powerful results (or both).

The monograph is divided into five chapters. Chapter 1 provides information on the data that researchers use, the types of questions addressed, and the variables used to test these questions. We also detail some of the limitations of these variables. Chapters 2, 3, and 4 focus on sources that potentially compromise analyst independence—incentives in the sell-side analyst's environment, selectivity on the part of analysts, and analysts' cognitive biases (Chapter 2); corporate clients (Chapter 3); and other analysts (Chapter 4). Chapter 5 summarizes the key inferences drawn from the research on each of these sources and provides some thoughts as to what the future may hold.

We would like to thank CFA Institute for funding. The assistance of Anne Higgs and Xin Wang is also gratefully acknowledged.

1. Security Analysts' Forecasting Behavior

To gain some notion of the quality of security analysts' earnings forecasts, researchers typically analyze properties of the earnings estimates and analysts' stock recommendations. The four most widely studied forecast properties are bias, accuracy, dispersion, and newsworthiness. Our objectives in this chapter are to describe how researchers typically measure these properties, to summarize the types of questions they address with each measure, to present descriptive data on these properties for 1980–2002, and to describe certain limitations of these measures as proxies for the constructs they purportedly capture. Our overriding goal is to provide the reader with a benchmark for interpreting the research, summarized in subsequent chapters, that analyzed one or more of these properties.

Forecast Properties

Researchers use common proxies to capture bias, accuracy, dispersion, and newsworthiness in the context of analysts' forecasts. Note, before we move on, that none of these properties imply the existence of any other proxy; that is, the "least biased" forecasts, for example, need not be the "most accurate" or the "most newsworthy." In addition to defining the properties and discussing their proxies in this section, we discuss the major questions researchers use each property to answer.

Bias. Bias refers to whether and to what degree analysts' forecasts are skewed above or below the "true" value of the number being forecasted. Although bias can be calculated for any forecasted item—earnings forecasts, stock recommendations, or price targets—it is most easily measured for earnings forecasts because earnings pertain to a defined period (a fiscal quarter or year), are calculated by using a set of agreed-upon rules (in studies of U.S. data, U.S. generally accepted accounting principles, GAAP), are audited by an external party and subject to the monitoring and enforcement functions of the U.S. Securities and Exchange Commission (SEC), and are reported by the company on a timely basis (usually in quarterly earnings announcements). Determining what the bias is in a stock recommendation is less straightforward because recommendations often do not specify a precise targeted return (they provide only a directional prediction, such as "the stock will outperform the market") and because the horizon over which the recommendation pertains is not precisely defined. Price targets avoid the first of these limitations (imprecision as to the expected target value), but they suffer from the same timing disadvantage that stock recommendations do.[1]

To define the bias in analysts' earnings forecasts, researchers use the forecast error, *FE*. It is typically calculated as the difference between company *j*'s reported earnings per share (EPS) for quarter q, $A_{j,q}$, and the analyst's forecast of company *j*'s EPS for quarter q issued at time t, $F_{j,q,t}$; that is,

$$FE_{j,q,t} = A_{j,q} - F_{j,q,t}. \tag{1.1}$$

Usually, the researcher scales the difference between the forecasted and reported earnings number by some variable to express the forecast error as a percentage. This scaling is done to aggregate forecast errors for companies of different sizes. In particular, because large companies tend to have larger EPS than small companies, combining data from companies of different sizes without some scaling is statistically problematic.

In general, research has produced similar results when various scaling variables were used. Share price tends to be the preferred scaling variable because it leads to fewer outlier concerns than do scaling variables based on EPS. Scaling variables based on EPS are much more likely to take on small values (which causes the ratio to become extremely large). Share price is typically measured at a time prior to the date that the analyst issued a forecast (e.g., the price 10 calendar days before the forecast issued on day t, denoted $P_{j,t-10}$). Measuring stock price prior to the date of the forecast issuance ensures that the stock price is not affected by the news in the forecast itself. The next most common scalar is the absolute value of the forecast, $|F_{j,q,t}|$. Using the absolute value of the forecast (rather than the signed value of the forecast) in the denominator preserves the direction of the forecast error indicated by the numerator.

Forecast errors will depend on which measure of reported earnings is used as the proxy for actual earnings, $A_{j,q}$. In their income statements and press releases announcing earnings, companies often report more than one earnings

---

[1]To see the timing problem, consider an analyst who issues a buy recommendation and a price target of $25 for a stock currently trading at $20 a share. The horizon for both the recommendation and the target price is near term (i.e., 6–12 months). For purposes of this example, ignore market movements that would affect the company's stock price; these moves only complicate the measurement of bias. Suppose further that 6 months after these forecasts are made, the company's stock price has declined to $18; after 12 months, it has increased to $27. Relative to the 6-month-price benchmark, both the target price and the stock recommendation are optimistic; relative to the 12-month target, the recommendation appears correct whereas the target price appears pessimistic.

number— to name just a few, earnings before extraordinary items; earnings after extraordinary items; earnings before discontinued items; primary EPS; diluted EPS; earnings before interest, taxes, and depreciation; and earnings before special items and comprehensive income. In choosing which earnings number to use as the benchmark, the researcher typically selects the actual earnings number that is most closely tied, conceptually, to the earnings construct that the analyst is forecasting. We revisit this issue of the "definitional consistency" of reported earnings and forecasted earnings in later sections.

In summary, the most common measure of bias in analysts' forecasts is the difference between the analyst's forecast of quarterly earnings and the actual EPS (primary, before extraordinary items), scaled by either share price 10 days prior to the forecast date,

$$FE_{j,q,t} = \frac{A_{j,q} - F_{j,q,t}}{P_{j,t-10}} \tag{1.2}$$

or by the absolute value of the forecast itself,

$$FE_{j,q,t} = \frac{A_{j,q} - F_{j,q,t}}{|F_{j,q,t}|}. \tag{1.3}$$

For both forecast-error measures, a negative value indicates optimism in the analyst's forecast (because the analyst predicted a higher value of earnings than was realized) and a positive value indicates pessimism (because the analyst's forecast was below the actual earnings realized). The more negative (positive) the forecast error, the more optimistic (pessimistic) the forecast.

Researchers are interested in bias primarily because it is believed to capture how analysts' forecasting behavior is influenced by the analysts' cognitive biases and by incentives provided by other parties that may influence the independence of the analyst. If analysts are both rational in their processing of information and truthful in their reporting of that information, one would expect analysts' forecasts, on average, to exhibit zero bias. (This is not to say that all analysts would be expected to predict actual earnings with zero error but, rather, that one would expect a roughly equal number of forecasts to overestimate earnings as underestimate earnings.) If analysts are not fully rational in their processing of information, however, or if their independence is compromised because they are encouraged (explicitly or implicitly) to report untruthfully, one would not expect the distribution of (signed) forecast errors to be centered at zero. As we will show in a later section, the bulk of empirical evidence indicates that analysts' forecasts tend to exhibit an optimism bias. That is, on average, analysts' forecast errors tend to be negative (i.e., forecasted earnings numbers are larger than actual earnings numbers).

Accuracy. Forecast accuracy captures the precision of the analyst's forecast. Precision is typically measured as how far the forecast deviates, in either direction, from the benchmark or target. Similar to bias, accuracy can, in theory, be calculated for any attribute forecasted by analysts; it is most easily calculated, however, for earnings forecasts (for the same reasons mentioned for forecast bias).

Because accuracy is concerned with only how far the forecast deviates from the actual value (not the direction in which it deviates), measures of accuracy focus on the absolute value of the forecast error, $|FE_{j,q,t}|$, or the squared value of the forecast error, $FE_{j,q,t}^2$. These unsigned measures abstract from whether the analyst's forecast is too high or too low (relative to reported earnings) and focus on how far the analyst's forecast is from the actual earnings number. Thus, forecast accuracy views a forecast of EPS that is $0.25 above actual earnings as being as inaccurate as an EPS forecast that is $0.25 below actual earnings. [Note, however, that when forecast accuracy is measured by price-scaled absolute (or squared) forecast errors, the same $0.25 deviation will be viewed as more accurate for a stock with a share price of $30 than for a stock with a share price of $10.]

Researchers are interested in forecast accuracy for several reasons. First, because analysts' earnings forecasts capture sophisticated users' expectations of earnings based on timely information, analyst forecast accuracy is believed to be an important determinant of the accuracy of the market's expectation of earnings. Thus, forecast accuracy proxies for the accuracy of the market's expectations (see, for example, Fried and Givoly 1982; O'Brien 1988). Second, researchers are interested in forecast accuracy in its own right (that is, not as a proxy for something else) because forecast accuracy provides a measure of how well analysts perform one aspect of their jobs—forecasting targets, such as earnings.[2] Researchers also use forecast accuracy as a criterion to evaluate whether particular disclosures or changes in accounting rules facilitate analysts' forecasting task; for example, did analysts' forecasts become more accurate following the change in the rules for reporting the performance of business segments?

---

[2]Evidence that forecast accuracy is an important factor affecting analysts' behavior is provided by Mikhail, Walther, and Willis (1999), who showed that analyst turnover (that is, a change in employer) is higher for analysts whose forecast accuracy is lower that that of their peers. If analysts are averse to turnover, this finding suggests that they are penalized for issuing forecasts that are inaccurate relative to the forecasts made by their peers.

A substantial body of research shows that analysts' earnings forecasts are more accurate than earnings forecasts generated by mechanical time-series models (e.g., Brown, Griffin, Hagerman, and Zmijewski 1987; O'Brien).[3] This result is perhaps not surprising given that, at a minimum, the mechanical models are available to analysts and could be used by them. Stated differently, how could analysts' forecasts not be *at least as* accurate as forecasts from a simple time-series model? A finding that analysts' forecasts are less accurate than a mechanical model's forecasts would suggest that analysts destroy value relative to what an investor could glean from a statistically generated forecast of earnings. Such value destruction seems implausible in light of the size of the security analyst industry and the amount of dollars that support the industry and is inconsistent with what has been observed.

Further work has shown that the greater superiority of analysts' forecasts is attributable to a timing advantage and to an informational advantage. In particular, Brown, Griffin, Hagerman, and Zmijewski showed that the superiority of analysts' forecasts relative to forecasts made from time-series models is a result of (1) analysts' better use of information existing on the date that the time-series data are known (an information advantage) and (2) analysts' better use of information that arrives after this date but before actual earnings are reported (a timing advantage).

Forecast accuracy is also used as a criterion in assessing whether and how analysts' forecasting behavior is affected by aspects of the forecasting task itself, features of the company's information environment, and attributes of the analyst or the analyst's work environment. Research shows that analysts' earnings forecasts are less accurate when the forecasts are made early in the fiscal year (that is, when the forecasts are older as measured by the number of days they precede the earnings announcement date; see O'Brien) and when actual earnings turn out to be a reported loss (e.g., Brown 2001; Hwang, Jan, and Basu 1996). In terms of features of the company's information environment, research shows that small companies, companies with relatively unpredictable earnings, and companies that are complex (as measured by the number of lines of business) result in less accurate analyst earnings forecasts (Brown, Richardson, and Schwager 1987). In terms of properties of the analyst and the work environment, research has examined whether more experienced

---

[3]By "mechanical model," we mean a time-series model of earnings that is determined by patterns existing in the company's historical earnings series. The simplest such model is a random walk, which posits that the best predictor of next year's earnings is this year's earnings. Another commonly used mechanical model is a seasonal random walk model. This model is typically applied to quarterly earnings and holds that the best predictor of earnings for quarter t is earnings in quarter $t - 4$.

analysts have more accurate forecasts than less experienced analysts (Mikhail, Walther, and Willis 1997) and whether properties of the analyst's work environment affect analyst accuracy (Clement 1999; Jacob, Lys, and Neale 1999).

Dispersion. Both bias and accuracy are properties of individual analysts' forecasts; that is, they can be calculated for each forecast that an analyst issues. In contrast, dispersion is a property of the distribution of the many forecasts prevailing at a point in time. Dispersion describes the variation among analysts' beliefs about a given company's future performance. It is often used as a proxy for the degree of heterogeneity of beliefs in the market: The greater the dispersion in analysts' forecasts, the less the consensus about what earnings will be.

The two most common statistics for capturing variation among forecasts are the standard deviation of analysts' forecasts and the coefficient of variation of those forecasts. The standard deviation of analysts forecasts for company *j*'s quarter q earnings, $\sigma(F_{j,q})$, is the sum of the squared deviations of each forecast value from the average forecast value:

$$\sigma(F_{j,q}) = \sqrt{\sum_{n=1}^{N} \left(F_{j,q,t} - \overline{F_{j,q}}\right)^2}, \tag{1.4}$$

where $\overline{F_{j,q}}$ is the average of the N individual analysts' forecasts of company *j*'s quarter q earnings. The coefficient of variation, CV, is the standard deviation expressed as a fraction of the mean forecast:[4]

$$CV(F_{j,q}) = \frac{\sigma(F_{j,q})}{\overline{F_{j,q}}}. \tag{1.5}$$

Larger values of $\sigma(F_{j,q})$ and $CV(F_{j,q})$ indicate greater dispersion.

Researchers' interests in dispersion focus on the ability of this measure to proxy for the strength, or degree of heterogeneity, of market participants' beliefs about earnings expectations and on dispersion as a direct measure of the difficulty of the forecasting task. Specifically, greater forecast dispersion is believed to reflect both more weakly held beliefs and a more difficult forecasting

---

[4]The coefficient of variation has advantages and disadvantages as a measure of dispersion. Its main advantage is that it controls for differences in scale that might arise in comparisons of dispersion for different companies or samples (for example, in comparing the dispersion of analysts' forecasts for IBM Corporation with the dispersion of forecasts for Xicor). Its main disadvantage is that it is not defined if the mean forecast is negative. For the most part, research generally has found that the coefficient of variation and standard deviation behave similarly as measures of dispersion.

task. Research shows, consistent with the task difficulty thesis, that companies with more unpredictable time series of past earnings have greater forecast dispersion than companies with highly predictable earnings series.

Newsworthiness. Newsworthiness captures the amount of information conveyed by the analyst's forecast; in academic research, this construct is often referred to as the "information content" of an event. The amount of news conveyed by an analyst's forecast can be measured in several ways, including reference to the forecasted item itself and reference to market movements. We consider each news measure in turn.

For news captured by the content of the forecast itself, researchers have measured the "surprise" in the analyst's forecast by the extent to which the forecast deviates from the consensus forecast (that is, $F_{j,q,t} - \overline{F_{j,q}}$) or from the same analyst's forecast issued at some earlier date $t - \tau$ (that is, $F_{j,q,t} - F_{j,q,t-\tau}$). Both measures can be thought of as measures of the amount of *revision* in the analyst's forecast. Researchers sometime refer to the revision measure based on the consensus forecast as a measure of the "boldness" of the analyst's forecast, with bold forecasts reflecting larger deviations from consensus forecasts than tentative forecasts reflect. As with forecast errors, measures of forecast revision and boldness are typically divided by share price to remove scale effects in the data and to facilitate aggregation across a broad sample of companies. All else being equal, researchers expect bold forecasts and forecasts containing large revisions from the analyst's previous forecast to be associated with larger changes in market expectations than are tentative forecasts and forecasts that reiterate prior forecast information.

Some measures of newsworthiness that have been suggested are related to market movements. That is, the news in the forecast is captured by changes in market expectations, as reflected in the company's stock price movement around the forecast release date. Forecasts that convey large amounts of favorable (unfavorable) information should be associated with large positive (large negative) movements in stock prices. Implicit in these indirect measures of forecast news is that by measuring the price reaction over a narrow window of time centered on the forecast disclosure date, the researcher identifies the stock price movement that is uniquely associated with the news in the analyst's forecast. Of course, whether the assumption of uniqueness is reasonable depends on whether other disclosures or events occurred at the same time as the analyst's forecast. Common concurrent disclosures include earnings announcements (Stickel 1989 showed that analyst forecast activity increases in response to earnings announcements) and other analysts' reports (some research suggests that analyst forecast activity resembles "herd" behavior; we review the herding literature in Chapter 4).

Researchers are interested in the newsworthiness of analysts' forecasts for several reasons. First, revisions in analysts' forecasts are often used as a proxy for how *individual* market participants respond to a given event or disclosure. These types of analyses complement research that examines how *aggregate* market behavior (as reflected in stock prices) responds to the same event. Second, measures of the newsworthiness of analysts' forecasts provide assessments of the "value added" by analysts. If analysts' forecasts contain abundant new information about earnings, researchers would expect to observe large values (positive and negative) of revision activity and boldness. By examining the market reactions to forecasts, researchers can assess the extent to which investors believe that analyst forecasts convey new information.

Within this second body of literature (on the value added by analysts), research has shown that investors react in the predicted manner to the news in analysts' earnings forecasts. Positive (negative) price reactions can be observed in response to good (bad) news, with the extent of the price movement increasing in accord with the amount of the news conveyed by the analyst report (e.g., Brown, Foster, and Noreen 1985; Givoly and Lakonishok 1979; and Lys and Sohn 1990). For example, reports containing larger (smaller) revisions in EPS forecasts are generally met with larger (smaller) price responses.

Research has shown that other elements of analysts' reports, such as stock recommendations, also convey news, as indicated by upward (downward) price movements following revisions to buy or strong buy (to sell or strong sell) recommendations (e.g., Elton, Gruber, and Grossman 1986; Womack 1996). Research on the relative effects of the news in stock recommendations and the news in earnings forecast revisions has indicated that these elements of the analyst's report separately influence stock returns (Francis and Soffer 1997). Finally, a recent study by Asquith, Mikhail, and Au (forthcoming 2004) found that the qualitative justifications that analysts include in their reports to support their earnings forecasts are at least as important in terms of news content as stock recommendations.

In short, research has found that analysts' reports, taken as a whole or in individual components, move share prices in the predicted directions.

Extending this literature, researchers have attempted to use tests of market reactions to discern whether investors "see through" some lack of independence on the part of an analyst. In this approach, the research design partitions market reactions to forecasts by the extent of the independence of the analyst issuing the forecast. The objective is to assess whether "affiliated" analysts' forecasts (that is, forecasts made by analysts who have strong ties with the followed company, such as those created by underwriting or investment banking relationships) are associated with different market responses from the forecasts of unaffiliated analysts following the same company. Most research studying these differences has found weaker reactions to affiliated analysts' forecasts, which suggests that investors discount the news conveyed by affiliated analysts' forecasts. Thus, investors may indeed recognize at least some of the security analyst's dependence on employer ties. We describe this research in Chapter 2.

Evidence on Forecast Properties, 1980–2002

To gain a better sense of the four previously discussed properties of analysts' forecasts, we calculated measures of bias, accuracy, dispersion, and newsworthiness for all analysts' EPS forecasts available in the Zacks Investment Research database in 1980–2002.

Bias. Turning first to bias, we calculated the signed realized forecast error for analyst i's year t forecast for company j (adjusted for stock splits and stock dividends) as

$$FE_{j,q,t} = A_{j,q} - F_{j,q,t}, \qquad (1.6)$$

where $A_{j,t}$ is company j's year t EPS before discontinued operations, extraordinary items, and the cumulative effects of any accounting changes (Compustat annual data item #58) and $F_{i,j,t}$ is analyst i's year t forecast for company j.

To aggregate forecast errors across companies of different sizes, we scaled by share price 10 trading days before the Zacks forecast release date. This calculation yielded a price-deflated measure of forecast bias:

$$\begin{aligned}
Bias_{j,q,t} &= FE_{j,q,t} \\
&= \frac{A_{j,q} - F_{j,q,t}}{P_{j,t-10}}.
\end{aligned} \qquad (1.7)$$

We also scaled by the absolute value of the forecast, and this calculation yielded a forecast-deflated measure of forecast bias:

$$\begin{aligned}
Bias_{j,q,t} &= FE_{j,q,t} \\
&= \frac{A_{j,q} - F_{j,q,t}}{|F_{j,q,t}|}.
\end{aligned} \qquad (1.8)$$

Because analysts' forecasts differ by the horizon of earnings being forecasted, we report results in terms of years—current-year earnings (fiscal year t, denoted FY0), one-year-ahead earnings (year $t + 1$, FY1), and two-year-ahead earnings (year t + 2, FY2). For current-year forecasts, we also distinguished between forecasts based on their age, with age measured as the number of calendar days between the forecast release date and the FY0 earnings announcement. We separately examined the "most current FY0" forecasts (i.e., those less than 90 days old). In total, the sample consisted of 940,014 forecasts of FY0 earnings (of which 162,456 were most current), 593,879 FY1 forecasts, and 35,034 FY2 forecasts. The descriptive evidence about forecast optimism gleaned from this study is presented in **Table 1.1**.

In Table 1.1, the mean price-scaled and forecast-scaled forecast errors for all forecasts are reliably *negative*, indicating that, on average, analysts' earnings forecasts were optimistic over this sample period. For example, for FY0 forecasts, on average, the earnings forecasted (scaled by forecast) were overly optimistic by 92.53 percent (Panel B) or about 2.48 percent of share price (Panel A). The large mean values for the forecast-scaled forecast errors in Panel B suggest the presence of small EPS figures in the sample.[5]

Table 1.1 also reveals that the extent of optimism increases with a lengthening forecast horizon: FY2 forecast errors are significantly more optimistic than those for FY1 (the difference is –122.26 percent versus –97.91 percent). FY1 forecasts are themselves more optimistic than FY0 forecasts, which in turn, are more optimistic than the most current FY0 forecasts. All differences in Table 1.1. are significant at the 10 percent level.

Panel C of Table 1.1 presents evidence on the pervasiveness of analyst optimism as captured by the percentage of observations for which the forecast error was negative.[6] Again, the optimism of analysts' forecasts as a percentage of forecasts increases with the horizon for which the forecast is being made. Consistent with the newest forecasts showing the least optimism, the frequency of negative forecasts errors in the most current FY0 category is 60.7 percent, significantly less than the 68.8 percent reported for all FY0 forecasts.

Based on recent evidence (described in Chapter 3) that suggests changes in the patterns of optimism in analysts' forecasts over time, we also examined trends in annual mean forecast errors. Specifically, using the data in Table 1.1, we estimated a simple regression of forecast errors on a trend variable, *Trend$_t$*, which was calculated as *Year t* – 1979. The regression equation is

$$FE_{j,q,t} = \alpha_0 + \alpha_1 Trend_t + e_{j,q,t},\tag{1.9}$$

where $e_{j,q,t}$ is the residual. The results of this analysis are shown in **Table 1.2**.

---

[5]That is, $0.02 of forecast bias represents a large proportion of the forecast when expected EPS are small and/or when actual earnings are negative. For example, suppose actual earnings are –$0.05 per share and forecasted earnings are $0.02 per share. The forecast-scaled forecast error for this observation will be $(-0.05 - 0.02)/|0.02| = -350\%$.

[6]Note that because the denominator in the scaled forecast-error metric is always positive, regardless of whether one uses the stock price or the absolute value of the earnings forecast, measures of pervasiveness are the same for the price-scaled and the absolute-forecast-scaled measures of bias. Stated differently, pervasiveness is determined by the sign of the numerator, which is the same for all measures of signed forecast errors.

Table 1.1. Descriptive Data on Signed Forecast Errors, 1980–2002

Year	A. Mean Forecast Bias Scaled by Price				B. Mean Forecast Bias Scaled by Forecast				C. Forecasts Biased Upward			
	Most Current FY0	All FY0	FY1	FY2	Most Current FY0	All FY0	FY1	FY2	Most Current FY0	All FY0	FY1	FY2
1980	0.0000	−0.0088	−0.0319	−0.0777	0.0060	−0.0774	−0.2278	−0.4230	43.4%	52.4%	72.7%	91.4%
1981	−0.0002	−0.0142	−0.0618	−0.0675	−0.0092	−0.1742	−0.4404	−0.5208	43.9	64.5	87.6	81.8
1982	−0.0057	−0.0289	−0.0590	−0.0566	−0.0239	−0.6756	−0.5048	−0.4445	56.5	76.1	83.0	87.3
1983	−0.0073	−0.0181	−0.0361	−0.0638	−0.5310	−0.5850	−0.3761	−0.5218	56.6	66.3	79.3	87.0
1984	−0.0119	−0.0244	−0.0585	−0.0823	−0.1592	−0.5039	−0.5414	−0.6899	58.1	69.0	84.3	90.5
1985	−0.0160	−0.0313	−0.0576	−0.0576	−0.4287	−0.8816	−0.7854	−0.4875	56.9	72.9	85.0	88.2
1986	−0.0156	−0.0298	−0.0332	−0.0424	−0.5759	−0.9953	−0.4661	−0.3764	56.5	70.0	75.7	75.3
1987	−0.0115	−0.0168	−0.0224	−0.0410	−0.6210	−0.4802	−0.2878	−0.5789	52.8	60.4	64.4	76.7
1988	−0.0101	−0.0156	−0.0313	−0.0569	−0.1421	−0.2213	−0.3372	−0.5959	53.3	56.9	71.4	85.5
1989	−0.0089	−0.0210	−0.0449	−0.0635	−0.1269	−0.3072	−0.5878	−0.8674	56.8	66.4	82.3	88.2
1990	−0.0149	−0.0287	−0.0551	−0.0632	−0.2547	−0.4866	−0.6709	−0.8267	59.2	70.4	85.6	92.2
1991	−0.0175	−0.0287	−0.0467	−0.0546	−0.4451	−0.6674	−0.6823	−0.6918	59.9	71.3	84.1	89.6
1992	−0.0168	−0.0259	−0.0368	−0.0387	−0.5094	−0.6997	−0.5775	−0.5390	57.3	69.0	80.9	84.2
1993	−0.0158	−0.0216	−0.0246	−0.0396	−0.7383	−0.6654	−0.4036	−0.6443	59.4	67.2	73.7	79.2
1994	−0.0105	−0.0145	−0.0297	−0.0450	−0.4345	−0.3318	−0.4413	−0.5130	50.8	57.5	70.7	77.7
1995	−0.0104	−0.0207	−0.0346	−0.0561	−0.2941	−0.5456	−0.4627	−0.7686	55.1	64.9	74.3	86.1
1996	−0.0124	−0.0194	−0.0354	−0.0599	−0.4302	−0.5381	−0.7001	−1.1136	56.5	64.2	77.9	88.0
1997	−0.0138	−0.0217	−0.0409	−0.0531	−0.4181	−0.6746	−0.8616	−1.1406	58.4	66.9	83.7	87.9
1998	−0.0166	−0.0263	−0.0342	−0.0477	−0.5412	−0.8354	−0.6760	−1.1699	66.9	75.3	79.1	82.8
1999	−0.0146	−0.0183	−0.0336	−0.0553	−0.3878	−0.4924	−1.0267	−2.3406	65.7	67.1	75.1	87.5
2000	−0.0180	−0.0245	−0.0519	−0.0519	−0.9893	−2.0920	−3.4797	−2.3866	68.7	71.8	86.6	90.2
2001	−0.0331	−0.0440	−0.0538	−0.0487	−2.0055	−2.6262	−2.2908	−1.5032	77.3	82.3	83.1	82.5
2002	−0.0308	−0.0377	−0.0292	—	−1.5105	−1.8806	−1.7650	—	74.1	75.0	74.2	—
Average for period	−0.0158	−0.0248	−0.0401	−0.0526	−0.6194	−0.9253	−0.9791	−1.2226	60.7%	68.8%	79.0%	85.8%

FY = fiscal year.

Table 1.2. Trends in Signed Forecast Errors over Time, 1980–2002

Statistic	Most Current FY0	All FY0	FY1	FY2
Intercept	−0.0035	−0.0177	−0.0466	−0.0656
t-Statistic	−1.56	−5.50	−9.06	−14.66
Trend	−0.0008	−0.0005	0.0005	0.0009
t-Statistic	−5.20	−2.08	1.23	2.55

We report the point estimates for the intercept, $\hat{a}_0$, which reflects the average signed forecast error over the sample period, after the trend was controlled for, and for the slope coefficient on *Trend*, $\hat{a}_1$, which reflects the average trend per year in forecast errors. Note first that the intercept values are consistent with those in Table 1.1; that is, on average, all forecast horizons indicate optimism, with the degree of optimism increasing with the forecast horizon.

Turning next to the coefficient estimates on any trend variable, note that, although Table 1.2 provides some evidence of increases in optimism for FY0 forecasts over time, the trend reverses for FY1 and FY2 forecasts. The statistical significance of some of these trends indicates the trend is reliably different from zero (particularly for most current FY0 forecasts), but the economic significance of the trends is modest.[7]

Research has shown that the presence in the total pool of forecasts for companies that experienced losses has a dramatic effect on perceptions of bias in analysts' forecasts. In particular, Brown (2001), Dowen (1996), and Hwang et al. found that forecasts for companies that experienced losses during the year ("loss companies") are more optimistic than forecasts for companies that were profitable ("profit companies"). To see whether loss companies drive the optimism observed in Table 1.1, we partitioned the sample by whether the company reported a loss in year *t*. We report the results of this partitioning for FY0 forecast errors in **Table 1.3**. For purposes of this analysis (and all subsequent analyses described in this chapter), we focus on price-scaled forecast errors (the results for forecast-scaled metrics were similar in all respects).

The mean forecast errors reported in the bottom row of Table 1.3 make clear that, on average in our sample period, loss companies led to significantly more optimistic forecast errors (–9.36 percent of share price) than did profit companies (–0.94 percent of share price). That is, the average optimism we found for loss companies was 10 times the average optimism found for profit companies. The fraction of forecasts that were optimistic (pessimistic) is also significantly larger (smaller) for loss companies than for profit companies.

---

[7]As we describe in more detail in the section "Components of Forecast Errors," drawing conclusions about changes in optimism over time is difficult because of shifts over time in the definitions of "earnings" being forecasted and being reported as target earnings numbers.

Table 1.3. Signed Forecast Errors Partitioned by Loss, 1980–2002

Year	A. Profit Companies				B. Loss Companies			
	Mean *FE*	Optimistic	Pessimistic	*n*	Mean *FE*	Optimistic	Pessimistic	*n*
1980	−0.0069	51.9%	46.8%	6,911	−0.1199	82.6%	17.4%	121
1981	−0.0121	63.9	35.1	11,362	−0.1271	95.9	4.2	217
1982	−0.0197	74.9	23.7	14,845	−0.1423	91.9	8.0	1,211
1983	−0.0103	64.2	33.8	14,776	−0.1063	90.3	9.4	1,308
1984	−0.0130	67.0	30.7	15,958	−0.1796	96.8	3.1	1,173
1985	−0.0133	69.1	28.4	16,870	−0.1454	96.7	3.2	2,662
1986	−0.0093	65.2	32.4	19,151	−0.1392	95.6	3.8	3,585
1987	−0.0075	57.4	39.9	21,480	−0.1056	88.3	10.7	2,254
1988	−0.0060	53.8	43.4	28,989	−0.1230	91.7	8.1	2,575
1989	−0.0116	64.0	33.4	25,535	−0.1178	91.8	7.7	2,465
1990	−0.0126	66.9	30.0	30,128	−0.1463	96.0	3.6	4,139
1991	−0.0099	66.8	30.3	32,616	−0.1199	93.2	6.5	6,690
1992	−0.0081	63.5	33.3	38,341	−0.1081	94.7	4.9	8,286
1993	−0.0085	63.3	33.3	45,060	−0.0950	89.4	9.7	8,056
1994	−0.0057	53.8	42.8	51,031	−0.0837	87.2	12.3	6,453
1995	−0.0094	61.2	35.0	51,449	−0.0928	88.4	10.8	8,047
1996	−0.0074	60.2	36.3	54,198	−0.0854	86.3	12.6	9,895
1997	−0.0076	62.0	34.4	50,589	−0.0809	87.6	11.5	12,083
1998	−0.0105	71.2	26.1	48,454	−0.0822	90.0	9.3	13,701
1999	−0.0078	63.5	33.7	51,302	−0.0605	81.6	17.3	12,773
2000	−0.0089	66.3	31.1	47,838	−0.0674	87.1	12.3	17,408
2001	−0.0145	78.2	19.5	44,820	−0.0954	89.6	9.8	25,715
2002	−0.0096	69.1	28.0	46,340	−0.0992	88.0	11.1	21,154
Average for period	−0.0094	64.3%	32.7%	768,043	−0.0936	89.0%	10.3%	171,971

Note: Forecast errors scaled by price.

Finally, in unreported tests, we assessed whether the trend in forecast errors over time differs between loss and profit companies. We found no discernible trend in the mean forecast errors of profit companies but found a significant upward trend for loss companies. This result suggests that, over time, forecast errors of loss companies have become less optimistic.

Accuracy. Now consider forecast accuracy, which we measured as the absolute value of the signed price-scaled forecast error, $Acc_{j,q,t}$, which was calculated as

$$Acc_{j,q,t} = |FE_{j,q,t}|$$
$$= \left| \frac{A_{j,q} - F_{j,q,t}}{P_{j,t-10}} \right|. \tag{1.10}$$

Recall that this measure is an inverse measure of accuracy, so *larger* values indicate *less precise* forecasts. Mean values of *Acc* are shown for each of the four forecasts in **Table 1.4**. These results clearly show that absolute forecast errors increase as the forecast horizon increases. The increasing values indicate that analysts are less precise in forecasting earnings farther in the future.

We also probed the trend in forecast accuracy (not tabulated here). For both current forecasts (FY0) and one-year-ahead forecasts (FY1), we found weak evidence of an increasing trend; for FY2 forecasts, however, regression tests showed a significant decline, of about –0.0009 per year (significant at the 10 percent level). The decline in absolute forecast errors means that over the past 23 years, analysts have become, on average, more accurate at forecasting two-year-out earnings.

Table 1.4. Absolute Forecast Errors, 1980–2002

Year	Most Current FY0	All FY0	FY1	FY2
1980	0.0110	0.0224	0.0439	0.0808
1981	0.0126	0.0249	0.0669	0.0907
1982	0.0139	0.0356	0.0684	0.0653
1983	0.0135	0.0262	0.0455	0.0682
1984	0.0199	0.0324	0.0640	0.0883
1985	0.0227	0.0368	0.0630	0.0653
1986	0.0234	0.0363	0.0413	0.0531
1987	0.0193	0.0256	0.0379	0.0498
1988	0.0178	0.0271	0.0433	0.0635
1989	0.0169	0.0293	0.0515	0.0689
1990	0.0207	0.0353	0.0599	0.0672
1991	0.0225	0.0344	0.0522	0.0587
1992	0.0226	0.0316	0.0435	0.0464
1993	0.0208	0.0280	0.0341	0.0518
1994	0.0178	0.0239	0.0413	0.0544
1995	0.0162	0.0275	0.0438	0.0626
1996	0.0178	0.0263	0.0427	0.0654
1997	0.0188	0.0278	0.0470	0.0584
1998	0.0218	0.0321	0.0425	0.0577
1999	0.0205	0.0268	0.0454	0.0621
2000	0.0232	0.0319	0.0575	0.0569
2001	0.0367	0.0484	0.0604	0.0583
2002	0.0350	0.0437	0.0350	—
Total	0.0217	0.0319	0.0482	0.0596

Note: Forecast errors scaled by price.

Dispersion. Information about the dispersion of analysts' earnings forecasts is reported in **Table 1.5**. The data are for the standard deviation in (undeflated) earnings forecasts issued for FY0. For these tests, we restricted attention to companies that had at least five forecasts of FY0 in the Zacks database in year t, with t = 1980 . . . 2002. Table 1.5 shows that the number of companies meeting this requirement increased significantly from 1980 to 1998. For the entire sample period, the mean standard deviation of earnings forecasts was 0.5461 (median of 0.3694); therefore, given that for most distributions 94 percent of all observations fall within ±2 standard deviations from the mean, these data indicate that 94 percent of analysts' forecasts for a given company were within a mean value of about $1.09 (median of $0.74) per share.

Table 1.5.   Forecast Dispersion, 1980–2002

Year	Mean	Median	No. of Companies
1980	0.5136	0.3119	748
1981	0.5608	0.3901	992
1982	0.4995	0.3306	1,264
1983	0.4870	0.3116	1,467
1984	0.3802	0.2388	1,604
1985	0.4035	0.2533	1,636
1986	0.4185	0.2539	1,813
1987	0.4111	0.2365	1,977
1988	0.3164	0.1962	2,138
1989	0.3521	0.2046	2,046
1990	0.3676	0.1939	2,124
1991	0.3094	0.1821	2,261
1992	0.3008	0.1762	2,576
1993	0.2748	0.1620	2,895
1994	0.2346	0.1441	3,364
1995	0.2351	0.1531	3,511
1996	0.2421	0.1545	3,768
1997	0.2269	0.1415	4,033
1998	0.2491	0.1554	4,269
1999	0.2234	0.1411	4,067
2000	0.2464	0.1524	3,768
2001	0.2843	0.1718	3,312
2002	0.2062	0.1207	3,021
Average for period	0.5461	0.3694	10,135

Note: Forecast errors scaled by price.

When we inspected the results for individual years and conducted a trend analysis (not tabulated here) similar to that performed for forecast errors, we found declines in forecast dispersion from 1980 to 2002 (the downward trends in both mean and median dispersion measures were significant at the 1 percent level). These data suggest a trend over time toward increasing consensus in analysts' forecasts for a given company. In particular, at the start of the sample period, 94 percent of analysts' forecasts were within $1.02 per share of the mean estimate; by the end of the sample period, 94 percent were within $0.41 per share.

Newsworthiness. Finally, we documented the newsworthiness of analysts' reports in the 1980–2002 period. We measured newsworthiness as the absolute value of the market-adjusted return on the day the analyst report was issued. For all analyst reports in our sample for companies for which we also had stock return data, we calculated the mean and median returns on report days and then aggregated the means and medians by year and in total. The results are reported in **Table 1.6**. The trend in newsworthiness in this period is evident from the data. In addition, we regressed the mean (and median) values of the absolute return on *Trend*. For mean absolute returns, the average increase in market reactions was 0.12 percent a year, significant at the 10 percent level; for median absolute returns, the yearly increase was smaller (0.06 percent a year) but still reliably different from zero at the 10 percent level. Thus, over the past 23 years, analysts' forecasts have conveyed increasingly more information to the market. This finding is consistent with the findings of Francis, Schipper, and Vincent (2002).

Section Summary. Our analyses of a large sample of analysts' earnings forecasts in the 1980–2002 period lead to the following conclusions: First, analysts' earnings forecasts are optimistic and the extent of optimism is greater for companies that have experienced losses in the current year than for profitable companies. The optimism increases as the forecast horizon increases. Second, over the 23-year sample period, we found
- no trend in optimism for current-year forecasts,
- a marked increase in the accuracy of farther-out earnings forecasts,
- a decline in dispersion, and
- a significant increase in the newsworthiness of analysts' forecasts.

Data Providers

As indicated by the definitions of forecast bias and forecast accuracy, studies examining analysts' forecast errors require a forecast measure and a measure of actual earnings. Research into the properties of analysts' earnings forecasts

Table 1.6. Newsworthiness of Analysts' Reports: Absolute Market-Adjusted Returns, 1980–2002

Year	Mean	Median
1980	0.0148	0.0107
1981	0.0145	0.0100
1982	0.0161	0.0110
1983	0.0152	0.0105
1984	0.0149	0.0097
1985	0.0144	0.0095
1986	0.0162	0.0108
1987	0.0192	0.0125
1988	0.0149	0.0099
1989	0.0139	0.0092
1990	0.0187	0.0117
1991	0.0192	0.0124
1992	0.0186	0.0118
1993	0.0180	0.0118
1994	0.0177	0.0113
1995	0.0176	0.0110
1996	0.0194	0.0120
1997	0.0261	0.0153
1998	0.0326	0.0187
1999	0.0362	0.0208
2000	0.0473	0.0274
2001	0.0426	0.0234
2002	0.0371	0.0198
Average	0.0220	0.0135

exploded with the availability of databases that provide information on these components. Although many of these databases provide forecasts of multiple attributes of a company's financial performance and provide up-to-date estimates that can be used as inputs into investing decisions, the discussion that follows focuses on the historical data typically used to calculate forecast errors. Historically, four databases—I/B/E/S, First Call, Zacks, and Value Line—have frequently been used for both forecast estimates and actual earnings. In addition to these providers of estimates, researchers have relied on Compustat for GAAP-based earnings and earnings components.

Because the validity of inferences drawn from measuring the properties of earnings forecast error depends on the appropriateness of the individual components of the metric, the characteristics of the data provided by the analyst-tracking services is an important consideration. One of the key attributes is the nature of earnings being forecasted. Analysts may estimate earnings on a basic or a diluted basis, and they may include or exclude various components of earnings, such as extraordinary items, discontinued operations, and nonrecurring and/or nonoperating items. These issues are important not only for research into individual analysts' forecasts but also for research that uses consensus forecasts. In particular, when compiling consensus forecasts, the analyst-tracking service must ensure that all analysts are forecasting earnings on a similar basis.

A key theme of this section is the importance of the comparability between measurement of the earnings forecast and measurement of the actual earnings number to the assessment of the properties of analysts' forecasts. The forecast and the actual earnings should be consistent in terms of the components of the earnings included. In addition, when a company has experienced stock splits or dividends, forecast and actual data must be presented on a consistent basis. In the remainder of this section, we summarize the main providers of data that are used in analyst-based research.

I/B/E/S. As one of the earliest sources of analyst data made publicly available, I/B/E/S (originally, Institutional Brokers Estimate System) is the data source for much of the research on analysts' forecasts. The firm of Lynch, Jones, and Ryan began to collect earnings estimates from the major brokerage firms in 1971. In July 1972, they printed the first I/B/E/S monthly consensus report. Only print reports were available until 1980, when the company offered its first electronic database. In 1986, Lynch, Jones, and Ryan and I/B/E/S were acquired by Citibank, and after a series of intermediate acquisitions, the Thomson Corporation acquired I/B/E/S in the fall of 2000. (Thomson also owns First Call.)

I/B/E/S produces summary consensus data (the Summary File) and detailed analyst-by-analyst records (the Detail File). The Summary File contains one record per company for each forecast period (fiscal year or quarter) for which forecasts were made. The file identifies the fiscal period and includes information on the number of estimates included in the consensus, the number of upward and downward revisions since the last report, the mean and median consensus estimates, the standard deviation of the estimates, and the high and low estimates. In addition, the Summary File indicates the date on which the summary statistics were calculated; this information allows one to assess the timeliness of the consensus measures. The Detail File contains individual-analyst estimates for as many as five FY periods and four quarterly forecasts and long-term growth estimates for each security followed. The file includes, among other information, an analyst code and a broker code, an indicator of the fiscal period being forecasted, the date of the estimate, and the earnings estimate itself.

I/B/E/S allows the majority of the analysts to dictate whether the forecast is reported as diluted EPS or basic EPS. If an analyst reports a forecast on a basis that is inconsistent with the majority of analysts reporting on a given company, I/B/E/S uses a dilution factor to make that analyst's estimate conform to the norm.[8] Typically, analysts reporting to I/B/E/S forecast diluted earnings on a "continuing operations" basis. Examination of the data also indicates that since at least 1998, most earnings data have been reported on a diluted basis (Brown and Sivakumar 2001, p. 7).

With regard to the nature of earnings, forecasts reported to I/B/E/S generally represent the analyst's forecast of earnings before the consideration of discontinued operations, extraordinary items, the cumulative effect of changes in accounting method, and other nonoperating items. I/B/E/S states:

> Earnings from operations means diluted earnings excluding all extraordinary items (specifically, those items defined by the accountants as extraordinary such as cumulative effect of an accounting change, early debt redemption, etc.), and excluding certain non-recurring, non-operating items (but not extraordinary by accounting definition) that a majority of the contributing analysts want to exclude (usually footnote items such as most restructuring charges, acquisition charges, or asset sales gains or losses). There is no "right" answer as to when a non-extraordinary charge is nonrecurring or non-operating and deserves to be excluded from the earnings basis used to value the company's stock. We believe the "best" answer is what the majority wants to use, in that the majority basis is likely what is reflected in the stock price. (I/B/E/S 2001, p. 7)

In addition to tracking analysts' estimates, I/B/E/S provides actual earnings for each fiscal period. The actual earnings numbers reported by I/B/E/S do not, however, represent a company's earnings as reported under GAAP. Rather, I/B/E/S attempts to adjust reported earnings so they are stated on a basis that is comparable to the basis on which analysts forecast earnings. By and large, the result is that actual earnings are reported after the effects of discontinued operations, extraordinary charges, and other nonoperating items have been removed. For this reason, earnings reported by I/B/E/S often disagree with a company's published actual earnings (e.g., earnings figures reported by Compustat).

---

[8]Analysts indicate whether they are forecasting basic or diluted EPS. If an analyst's forecast is received with a different indicator from the one the analyst used in the past, the Detail File adjusts it for consistency across time. In the Summary File, analysts' forecasts are adjusted to be on the same basis (basic or diluted) and so indicated in the database. I/B/E/S computes and stores a dilution factor for each company, which measures the difference between basic and diluted EPS. The dilution factor is based on the ratio of a company's last reported actual basic EPS to its last reported diluted EPS. If an individual analyst follows a company on a fully diluted (basic) basis whereas the majority of the analysts are forecasting basic (fully diluted) EPS, the one analyst's estimates are multiplied (divided) by the dilution factor. I/B/E/S provides the adjustment factor so that consensus forecasts can be obtained on either basis.

To maintain consistency and comparability among estimates, I/B/E/S employs a staff to examine forecasted and actual earnings for stock splits, extraordinary items, accounting changes, anomalies, and inconsistencies. In the event of a stock split, I/B/E/S immediately adjusts both current and historical estimates and actual data to consistently reflect the current capitalization. The dates of stock splits and the split factor are reported so users of the data can adjust the numbers back to their presplit levels if desired.[9]

First Call. First Call originated in 1984 as an electronic distributor of analyst meeting notes, and it began gathering and reporting earnings data in 1990. Similarly to I/B/E/S, First Call provides both summary and individual-analyst data. The summary data include (among other items) the end date of the fiscal period, the date on which the consensus forecast was calculated, the consensus mean and median earnings estimates, the standard deviation of the estimates, the number of estimates composing the consensus, the number of estimates raised and lowered since the last report, and the high and low forecasts. First Call computes new summary statistics each time a broker begins or ends coverage of a security, revises an estimate, or begins or ends participation in First Call's database. Only the most recent estimate made by each broker is used in the calculation of the summary statistics. Individual broker data include a number that identifies the broker, the fiscal-period end date, the date on which the estimate was made, the estimate itself, and the estimate source. The majority of estimates come from broker notes or via electronic transmission; other estimates come from weekly and monthly update files or through interaction with an analyst.

Earnings estimates and actual earnings from First Call are generally reported on a diluted basis. First Call reports both the forecasted and actual earnings after adjusting for items that the majority of analysts deem to be nonoperating and/or nonrecurring. (Items that qualify as extraordinary under GAAP standards are always excluded from earnings estimates and reported earnings.) Presumably, items that analysts include in their earnings forecasts are those analysts believe to be the most relevant for valuation

---

[9]Payne and Thomas (2002) investigated the use of I/B/E/S stock-split-adjusted data for the 1984–99 period. They reported that I/B/E/S stock-split adjustments have traditionally been rounded to the nearest penny (e.g., EPS of both $0.99 and $1.01 will be adjusted to $0.25 in a 4 to 1 stock split). Given the $0.25 postsplit EPS and the 4 to 1 adjustment factor, both EPS numbers would be adjusted back to $1.00. The authors noted that such rounding may have implications for research that uses split-adjusted earnings to calculate forecast errors.

purposes.[10] If analysts anticipate a significant nonextraordinary charge or gain that might be viewed as nonrecurring or nonoperating, their reports will often indicate whether they are including the item in (or excluding it from) their forecasts. From these disclosures, First Call ascertains the inclusion/exclusion decisions of the majority of the contributing analysts and prepares a footnote indicating the type of nonrecurring item, the size of the item, the period affected, and whether it was included or excluded by the majority of analysts.

First Call data also include a file with reported actual earnings. A corporation's actual reported earnings are adjusted to reflect the basis used by the majority of the analysts in their estimates. As a result, comparisons of actual earnings with forecasted earnings for a given company should be definitionally consistent. All forecasted and actual earnings numbers are adjusted for stock splits and dividends. The database contains information on the split factor so users of the data can convert numbers to a presplit basis if desired.[11]

In the fall of 2000, Thomson Corporation acquired I/B/E/S as part of its acquisition of Primark. Thomson maintained the I/B/E/S and First Call databases separately until 2002, when Thomson began to integrate the two databases. According to Chuck Hill, director of research at First Call, the historical data that carry forward into the single database will be the I/B/E/S data.

Zacks Investment Research. Zacks historical data for fiscal-year and long-term earnings growth estimates begin in 1978; for quarterly estimates, in 1981; and for stock recommendations and earnings surprises, in 1984. As I/B/E/S does, Zacks produces historical files of time-series data on a consensus (summary) basis and for individual analysts. For each fiscal period covered in the Summary File, the mean estimate, a 30-day consensus estimate, the standard deviation of the estimates, and the number of forecasts composing the consensus are provided. The file also reflects the number of analysts raising or lowering their forecasts since the publication of the last report. The Individual Estimate History File contains (among other variables) codes

---

[10]Using First Call footnote information, which provides details about which items are excluded and included from First Call forecasts, Gu and Chen (2003) examined the valuation implications of items that analysts choose to include/exclude from their forecasts. They noted, first, that both included and excluded items have increased in frequency and that the majority (approximately 64 percent) of both included and excluded items are losses. Their main tests showed that the items analysts keep in their forecasts are valued significantly more by investors than items they exclude from their forecasts. Their results suggest that analysts are successful in including the more value-relevant items and excluding items that are less relevant to investors.

[11]The rounding issue raised by Payne and Thomas with respect to I/B/E/S split adjustments is also a factor for First Call data, as documented by Baber and Kang (2002).

identifying the analyst and the broker who employs the analyst, the date of the analyst's forecast, the fiscal period for which the forecast was being made, the analyst's prior forecast, and the analyst's current forecast.

In response to interest in whether a company meets, beats, or misses the market's earnings expectation, Zacks developed the Earnings Surprise History File, a separate database that contains records specifically designed to facilitate assessments of earnings surprises. The records in this file include, among other items, company identification information, the fiscal-quarter-end data, the report date, the actual reported EPS, the consensus EPS estimate for the fiscal quarter as of the report date, and the earnings surprise.

Zacks documentation indicates that all per share data, estimated and actual, are provided on a primary basis. Although analysts may provide forecasts on a diluted basis, these data are converted by Zacks to primary equivalent shares prior to inclusion in the consensus. The Zacks individual estimate database is also maintained on a primary basis to facilitate analyst-to-analyst comparability. Zacks documentation further indicates that both earnings estimates and actual reported earnings are measures of earnings from continuing operations and are "maintained in conformance with a proprietary definition of operating EPS before extraordinary and nonrecurring and special items" (Zacks History Files 1999, p. 1) and are definitionally comparable. Zacks removes from earnings all items that qualify as extraordinary under Accounting Principles Board (APB) Opinion No. 30; they note, however, that many "unusual" items that do not qualify as extraordinary under APB No. 30 are also excluded from Zacks reports.

Zacks reports earnings forecasts and realizations on a consistent split-adjusted basis. This procedure ensures that forecast data are provided on a comparable basis through time in the event of a stock split or dividend. Zacks also produces unsplit data by reversing its cumulative split-adjustment process.

Value Line. Some researchers have used earnings estimate and actual earnings data from the *Value Line Investment Survey*. Value Line data were available in hard copy format long before I/B/E/S, Zacks, or First Call databases and, therefore, were used in some of the early research on analyst forecasting behavior. Value Line data are unique in that Value Line is not affiliated with any bank, broker, or insurance company. It does not sell securities or have any revenue source tied to securities transactions. The corporations whose stocks are covered compensate neither Value Line nor the individual analysts following the company. All Value Line revenues come from fees collected from subscribers. As a result of this independence, any bias in Value Line analyst forecasts cannot be attributed to analyst desires to attract revenue-generating business in the form of investment banking fees or brokerage commissions.

Another unique and desirable feature of Value Line data is the breadth of forecasts reported. When a Value Line analyst updates coverage of a given stock, the analyst provides annual estimates of many different measures, including sales, operating margins, net profit margin, tax rates, cash flows, capital investments, earnings, and dividends. Annual earnings forecasts are made for one and two years out, and a forecast is made of the average for the three-year to five-year time frame. In addition, Value Line continually revises and updates quarterly sales and earnings forecasts for the current year and one year out.

Offsetting these desirable features of Value Line forecasts are the selectivity in Value Line coverage and the lag between forecast dates and actual earnings report dates. Specifically, the *Value Line Investment Survey* is published weekly and covers approximately 1,700 stocks in more than 90 industries. The stocks selected by Value Line for coverage represent those stocks that Value Line believes are of the most interest to Value Line subscribers. Each week, on a predetermined schedule, Value Line prepares an in-depth analysis of about 130 companies in seven or eight industries. This rotating evaluation system results in forecasts for each company being updated once every 13 weeks. As a result, forecasts for some companies are as much as 13 weeks old at the time of the earnings release. Given that analysts' forecasts are known to contain more information as the announcement date nears (the timing advantage referred to previously), this lag probably reduces forecast accuracy.

Although Value Line does not dictate how analysts should treat different components of earnings, actual and forecasted EPS data generally exclude discontinued operations and extraordinary items and may also exclude nonrecurring items. With the forecasts, an analyst provides a commentary and footnotes, which frequently indicate the components of earnings included in the forecast (and, subsequently, in the actual reported earnings) and indicate whether the forecast is of basic or diluted EPS.

Compustat. Unlike the other databases reviewed, Compustat is not a source of analysts' forecasts but a source of (actual) reported earnings. We describe the earnings figures contained in Compustat because researchers often use Compustat data for the actual (reported) earnings numbers in their studies.

Compustat has traditionally reported basic and diluted EPS both before and after the effects of (as defined by GAAP) discontinued operations, extraordinary items, and the cumulative effect of accounting changes. Beginning in 1988, Compustat also began reporting "EPS from operations." Basic (diluted) operating EPS represents basic (diluted) EPS adjusted to remove the effects of all nonrecurring items, including the cumulative effect of accounting changes, discontinued operations, extraordinary items, special items, and nonrecurring items.

As of this writing, the combined Compustat quarterly and annual files report 14 variations of EPS, including various permutations of annual EPS as reported, 12-month moving EPS (EPS applicable to the last 12-month period), and EPS restated up to 10 years for acquisitions, accounting changes, discontinued operations, and/or stock splits/dividends occurring through the end of the most recent fiscal year.

A researcher's use of actual Compustat earnings data is appropriate only if the researcher believes that analysts are, in fact, attempting to forecast the particular Compustat measure of earnings.

Components of Forecast Errors

Researchers investigating questions that rely on measures of earnings forecast errors must be aware of the characteristics of both the earnings estimates and the actual reported earnings. Specifically, if analysts are forecasting a different form of earnings from that represented in the actual earnings number, the resulting forecast error will not be an appropriate measure of the earnings surprise. Such differences are compounded by within-analyst and across-analyst differences in the treatment of items to include/exclude from earnings and from shifts over time in what is included/excluded.

Skantz and Pierce (2000) showed that analysts do not always treat similar items consistently when forecasting earnings. In addition, over time, shifts in the nature of earnings being forecasted and reported may affect inferences drawn from longitudinal studies of forecast errors.

In this section, we summarize the results of research into how changes in the definition of earnings (used by analysts in forecasting earnings and by analyst-tracking services in determining the target earnings number being forecasted) affect inferences drawn from forecast errors. We then review research into how specific features of the distributions of forecast errors, depending on how and whether a researcher accounts for extreme observations in the data, might lead researchers to draw dramatically different conclusions.

Definitional Consistency. The apparent goal of most analysts whose forecasts appear in the databases examined by researchers is to forecast some measure of *operating* earnings. As the nature of the earnings number being forecasted has changed, the analyst-tracking services have responded by altering the actual reported EPS number to match the earnings being forecasted. Although the specifics differ by data provider, all three of the primary database providers acknowledge their efforts to focus on operating earnings in both their forecasts and reported actuals.

Numerous studies have documented differences between GAAP earnings numbers and earnings numbers reported by the analyst-tracking services (e.g., Abarbanell and Lehavy 2002; Bhattacharya, Black, Christensen, and Larson 2003; Bradshaw and Sloan 2002; Brown and Sivakumar). Several studies also documented an increase in the size of the difference between GAAP-based numbers and the earnings used by analyst-tracking services over time. These differences, and the trend in the size of the differences, appear to be the result of analyst-tracking services excluding an increasing number of charges from their reported earnings, effectively mimicking the exclusions being made by analysts and in corporate management *pro forma* earnings.

Separately, substantial evidence indicates that nonrecurring items have become more frequent in company financial statements (Abarbanell and Lehavy 2002; Bradshaw and Sloan; Collins, Maydew, and Weiss 1997; Elliott and Hanna 1996). This research also indicates that the incidence of negative special items far exceeds the incidence of positive special items.

Together, the increased frequency of special items and the increasing trend for analysts to exclude such items from their forecasts will result in an increasing gap between actual earnings as reported by analyst-tracking services and GAAP-based measures of earnings. Furthermore, because of the asymmetry in the frequency of negative versus positive special items (more negative than positive) and in their inclusion by analysts (analysts tend to exclude negative items more than they exclude positive items), we would expect to find increasingly negative differences between analysts' forecasts of earnings and GAAP-based measures of earnings. That is, we would expect that over time, analysts' forecasts would appear more optimistic than GAAP-based measures of earnings because of the increasing number of excluded negative items from the analysts' forecasts. Research supports this observation.

Brown and Sivakumar provided direct comparisons of three actual earnings measures—*Street* earnings (as captured by I/B/E/S actual earnings), *EDEP* (as measured by Compustat EPS before extraordinary items and discontinued operations), and *OPINC* (operating earnings defined as Compustat EPS adjusted to remove the effect of all special items). When all three measures of earnings are equal, nonrecurring and nonoperating items are absent. Over Brown and Sivakumar's full sample period, 1989–1997, the three measures agreed in more than 59 percent of the comparisons. When the data were examined year by year, however, the percentage of cases in which all three measures agreed declined significantly—from 64 percent in 1989 to 46 percent in 1997. The percentage of cases in which *OPINC* agreed with *EDEP* but not with *Street* increased from 21–27 percent prior to 1997 to 35 percent in 1997. Given that both *OPINC* and *EDEP* are Compustat numbers derived from information contained in SEC filings, this result suggests that analysts have increased their tendency to identify certain income as nonoperating or nonrecurring, even though identification of these nonoperating items is not available from SEC filings. Brown and Sivakumar also provided data on the magnitude of the differences in the three earnings measures. Consistent with the notion that the majority of nonoperating/nonrecurring items are negative, they found the mean and median values of *OPINC* and *Street* to be larger than those of *EDEP*.

Bradshaw and Sloan reported similar results for their comparison of quarterly *GAAP-EPS* (defined as Compustat EPS before extraordinary items and discontinued operations) and quarterly *Street-EPS* (defined as the actual EPS reported by I/B/E/S). In the 1985–90 period, these two measures of earnings were fairly close. After 1990 and through the end of their sample period in 1997, the two earnings measures diverged significantly, with *Street-EPS* exceeding *GAAP-EPS*. Furthermore, the authors reported that the magnitude and frequency of special items also increased over the 1985–97 period, with income-decreasing special items increasing at a more rapid rate than income-increasing items. Thus, similar to Brown and Sivakumar's findings, Bradshaw and Sloan found that both the greater incidence of negative special items and the increasing tendency for analyst-tracking services to exclude these items have contributed to an increasing gap between analysts' reported target numbers and targeted numbers tied to GAAP-based financial statements.

Over time, shifts in the components of earnings included in targeted earnings numbers have implications for research that uses these targets in calculating forecast errors. In particular, these shifts bear directly on research purporting to show that analysts have become less optimistic over time (e.g., Brown 2001; Matsumoto 2002). To test the possibility that the decline in forecast optimism is, in whole or in part, attributable to the use of adjusted earnings figures, Bradshaw and Sloan calculated forecast errors (by using both *Street-EPS* and *GAAP-EPS* as the measure of actual earnings) for subsets of their sample formed on the basis of the sign of the aggregate special items—positive, zero, negative. Their results showed that when a company recorded negative special items, the forecast error was negative (indicating optimism) and the level of optimism decreased over their sample period. They found the decline in optimism to be much more dramatic for forecast errors based on *Street-EPS*, however, than those based on *GAAP-EPS*. This finding is consistent with changes over time in the definition of *Street-EPS* (notably, the exclusion of negative special items) that would lead to *Street-EPS* being higher than *GAAP-EPS*. An important aspect of this study is that the subsets of zero and positive special items did not display any downward trend in forecast bias.

Abarbanell and Lehavy (2002; hereafter AL 2002) took issue with the conclusion that forecast optimism has declined in recent years. They argued that the changing definition of reported earnings used to calculate forecast errors has had a significant influence on these apparent trends. They extended the literature by examining the properties of the distribution of the difference between actual earnings as reported by Compustat and actual earnings as reported by the three primary analyst-tracking services (referred to as "forecast data providers" or FDPs). The FDPs were I/B/E/S, First Call, and Zacks. The difference between the two earnings constructs, Compustat earnings minus FDP earnings, was considered a measure of excluded items. Specifically, if Compustat earnings exceeded (were less than) FDP earnings, the difference was positive (negative) and excluded items were positive (negative) in aggregate.[12] AL (2002) focused on three properties of excluded items: tail asymmetry, the frequency of zeros and small values, and what they referred to as a "regime shift."

▓ *Tail asymmetry.* Focusing on 1992–1998 when data from all three FDPs were available, AL (2002) found that the distributions of excluded items had negative means, zero medians, and fatter and longer negative tails, regardless of the FDP used in the comparison. The negative tail represents observations for which FDP earnings exceeded Compustat earnings by extreme amounts. Further tests showed that observations in the extreme negative tail of the excluded-items distribution are associated with recognition of extremely negative special items (but not with extremely negative nonoperating items).

▓ *Frequency of zero earnings differences and systematic patterns in small differences.* AL (2002) showed that for all FDPs, median and modal values of excluded items in their sample period were zero. The zero modes indicate that FDP earnings were exactly the same as Compustat earnings in a large percentage of cases. The distributions also showed that as excluded items approached zero, Compustat earnings were more likely to exceed FDP earnings. Furthermore, the likelihood that excluded items would be negative (i.e., FDP earnings would be greater then Compustat earnings) increased as the absolute magnitude of the excluded items increased. The reason is the greater frequency and magnitude of extreme negative special items plus the fact that extreme negative special items are more likely to be added back to FDP earnings than to Compustat earnings. Both conditions increase the likelihood that the average value of excluded items will be negative.

---

[12]Compustat earnings exclude extraordinary items, discontinued operations, and the cumulative effect of accounting changes. Based on the documentation provided by the forecast databases, these items are also excluded from FDP earnings. Any difference between FDP earnings and Compustat earnings should, therefore, reflect above-the-line special, nonoperating, unusual items.

■ *Regime shift.* In examining intertemporal trends in excluded items, AL (2002) documented a regime shift in 1990. They showed that in I/B/E/S and Zacks data, the mean value of excluded items became significantly more negative (that is, FDP earnings > Compustat earnings) in 1990 and has remained more negative since then.[13] They described the significant change in 1990 as suggesting a pronounced regime shift.

AL (2002) also showed that the larger negative values after 1989 are attributable to (1) an increasing trend in both the number and magnitude of negative special items and (2) an increasing tendency for FDPs to exclude negative nonrecurring items from actual earnings.[14] In short, the two factors work together to cause the value of excluded items to appear more positive, giving the appearance of a decline in forecast optimism.

Error Distributions and Their Influence on Conclusions. In addition to research focused on the definitional consistency and shifts over time in how reported earnings are measured by analyst-tracking services, research has also probed whether and how properties of forecast-error distributions affect inferences about properties of these forecasts, such as bias. The key insight provided by this body of work is the dramatic effect that a small number of extreme observations may have on the overall conclusions to be drawn.

For the 1985–98 period, Abarbanell and Lehavy (2003); hereafter, AL (2003) documented the presence of two asymmetries (tail asymmetry and middle asymmetry) in the cross-sectional distribution of the forecast errors. *Tail asymmetry* is the presence of a longer, fatter negative tail than a positive tail (negative skewness); *middle asymmetry* is the presence of a higher occurrence of small positive forecast errors than small negative errors. Although the observations driving these asymmetries are a small percentage of the total number of observations, AL (2003) argued that the presence of both asymmetries is responsible, in part, for conflicting conclusions about analyst forecast bias.[15]

---

[13]First Call was excluded because its data were not available prior to 1992.

[14]The second factor is consistent with the findings of Philbrick and Ricks (1991), who quoted I/B/E/S as stating that 1989–1991 marked a period of significant cleanup of their data. AL (2002, p. 11) also referred to conversations with officials at Zacks and I/B/E/S that indicated "that the events of 1990 did cause procedural changes over the next year that were designed to align more closely the definition of earnings to be forecast by analysts to the definition of reported earnings employed by the FDPs."

[15]While acknowledging the presence of the tail and middle asymmetries, Cohen and Lys (2003) questioned whether the asymmetries are significant enough to affect the conclusions in prior research. In particular, they argued that the impact of the tail and middle asymmetries depends on the economic context and the statistical procedures used.

In particular, AL (2003) argued that whether a forecast-error distribution indicates forecast optimism depends on the statistic being considered. The *mean* forecast error is the measure most influenced by tail asymmetry; tail asymmetry causes the mean forecast error to be negative, which is suggestive of forecast optimism. If one focuses on the *pervasiveness* of bias, however, the higher incidence of small positive forecast errors than small negative errors in the middle asymmetry predominates and leads to a conclusion of pessimism. Finally, AL (2003) noted that the zero *median* forecast error (consistent with a lack of bias) is the result of the tail and middle asymmetries having offsetting results.

Regarding the impact of the asymmetries on analyst forecast bias, AL (2003) reported an untruncated forecast-error distribution with a mean of –0.126 (consistent with optimism) and a median of 0 (consistent with unbiased forecasts). These findings indicate that the negative (optimistic) tail of the distribution contains more extreme forecast errors of greater absolute magnitude than are found in the positive (pessimistic) tail. At the same time, positive forecast errors made up 48 percent of the distribution whereas negative (zero) forecast errors made up 40 percent (12 percent) of the observations. Examination of the distribution of forecast errors reveals that as the absolute forecast error approaches zero, one finds increasingly more small positive errors (a sign of pessimism) than small negative errors (a sign of optimism). This asymmetry alone would tend to drive means and medians toward small positive values, which would be interpreted as analyst pessimism.[16]

Some researchers take steps to deal with the presence of extreme forecast errors. For example, Keane and Runkle (1998) removed companies with large negative special items in reported earnings from their sample. Brown (2001) truncated large absolute forecast errors and reported a shift toward forecast pessimism in both the mean and median. Some researchers have used estimation procedures that place less weight on extreme observations (Basu and Markov 2003; Keane and Runkle). These alternative estimation procedures generally show less evidence of optimistic bias and less evidence of other forecasting behavior (such as underreaction to bad news) that are linked to optimism bias.

Section Summary. Recent research indicates that some conclusions regarding analyst forecasting behavior are sensitive to the tests and statistics chosen by the researcher; this sensitivity stems largely from the researcher's

---

[16]AL (2003) were not the first to recognize the presence of these asymmetries in the distribution of forecast errors. Degeorge, Patel, and Zeckhauser (1999) also observed that the optimistic mean forecast error is attributable to extreme negative forecast errors.

treatment of extreme values of forecast errors. The extreme values that are most influential are extreme negative forecast errors, which are both larger in magnitude and occur more frequently than extreme positive forecast errors. To a large extent, the greater incidence and magnitude of extreme negative forecast errors can be linked to the incidence of losses. That is, research has found significantly larger negative forecast errors for companies that have reported a loss than for profitable companies. Such extreme negative forecast errors may arise because losses are more difficult to predict than profits or because in the case of losses, analysts choose not to revise earlier forecasts to reflect the bad news. In this case, the earlier forecasts will be too high relative to the reported loss figures, generating the appearance of significant optimism in the early (but now stale) forecasts.

Regardless of what causes these extreme observations, the question remains of whether they are valid observations to be considered when determining characteristics of the overall distribution of forecast properties. When researchers view these observations as legitimate forecast observations (legitimate in the sense that they are not merely the result of some coding or input error), results show optimistic bias on average. When researchers view these observations as outliers to be excluded from the analysis, results depend on the time period studied and the test statistics used.

Summary and Conclusions

Researchers study many aspects of analysts' reporting behavior. In summarizing the behaviors, research often relies on statistics that capture selected quantitative components of the analyst's report. In particular, much attention has focused on attributes of analysts' earnings forecasts reflected in properties of the errors of those forecasts. Although research shows some sensitivity to how one measures these forecast errors (for example, care must be taken to make sure that the earnings estimate and the actual reported number used for comparison are definitionally consistent), for the most part, research has found the following:

- Analysts' earnings forecasts are, on average, optimistic; that is, they overstate the actual earnings number later reported by the company. Despite this bias, analysts' forecasts are more accurate than are forecasts derived from mechanical models of earnings.
- Both the degree of optimism in analysts' forecasts and the imprecision of the forecasts increase as the forecast horizon increases; that is, forecasts of farther-out earnings are more optimistic and less accurate than are forecasts of near-term earnings.

- Similarly, both the degree of optimism and imprecision are inversely related to the age of the forecast; that is, forecasts of annual earnings issued early in the fiscal year are more optimistic and less accurate than are annual forecasts issued closer to the earnings announcement date. This result is not surprising given that during the year, pieces of actual annual earnings are revealed through quarterly earnings realizations.
- Analysts' reports convey new information to the market, as evidenced by a significant stock price movement (adjusted for concurrent market movements) on the day a report is issued. Further evidence indicates that many components of the report (including revisions in earnings forecasts, revisions in stock recommendations, and the justifications for these revisions) contribute to explaining the movements in stock returns.
- Evidence of trends over time in the properties of analysts' forecasts is sensitive to the period examined (pre-1990 versus post-1990), the statistics calculated (mean versus median), and the treatment of extreme observations (included or excluded).

2. Explanations of Forecast Optimism

Numerous prior studies in academic accounting research have documented upward bias in sell-side analysts' earnings forecasts (e.g., Fried and Givoly 1982; O'Brien 1988). That is, research shows that analysts' forecasts of quarterly and annual earnings per share (EPS) tend to overestimate the EPS number subsequently announced by the company in its earnings announcement. These findings have intrigued academic accountants and drawn the attention of the U.S. Securities and Exchange Commission (SEC)—not because analysts seem to misestimate the earnings number later announced by the company but because analysts appear to systematically *overestimate* the subsequently announced earnings number. We refer to this phenomenon as "forecast optimism" or "optimistic forecasts."

Three general types of explanation have been offered for forecast optimism, which we label "incentive," "selection," and "cognitive" explanations. By far the most attention (from the popular press, regulators, and academic research) has been directed at incentives that come from analysts' employers. (Another type of incentive—pressure, real and imagined, from clients or potential clients—is discussed in Chapter 3.)

By *incentive* explanations, we mean incentives for optimism that are linked to aspects of the institutional environment in which the analyst works. Keep in mind that we focus on sell-side analysts.[17] Because the primary features of these environments relate to the analyst's role in securing or generating underwriting fees, investment banking business, and brokerage commissions, we consider these combined revenue-generating incentives as being associated with the analyst's employer because the employer benefits from these activities. Thus, the more an analyst's reporting behavior is unaffected by these incentives, the more we view that analyst as being independent of the employer; the more the analyst's forecasts appear to depend on these incentives, the more we characterize the analyst as exhibiting less independence from the employer.

In this chapter, we summarize the incentive, selection, and cognitive explanations and then present new evidence examining the combined ability of these potential factors to describe analyst forecast optimism. By examining

---

[17]For a discussion of buy-side analyst forecast bias and potential explanations of this bias, see Willis (2001).

these explanations simultaneously, the analysis extends prior studies that either ruled out alternative explanations for forecast optimism in the research design (e.g., Francis and Philbrick's 1993 use of Value Line data ruled out incentive explanations because Value Line does not perform underwriting, brokerage, or investment banking services) or assumed that other explanations are randomly distributed across the sample observations (e.g., Dugar and Nathan 1995; Lin and McNichols 1998).

After documenting that incentive, selection, and cognitive explanations are distinct phenomena affecting analyst forecast errors, we provide evidence on whether the intensity of these factors as explanations for forecast errors changed during the 1980–96 period. Evidence on changes over time in the ability of these explanations to account for forecast optimism is important because it sheds light on whether and how analysts' dependencies (on their employers, their own beliefs, and their own cognitive processing flaws) have changed over time.

Previous Research on the Explanations

The explanations for forecast optimism—incentives, selection, and cognitive biases—differ as to whether they assume the analyst is acting rationally or irrationally in the way she or he processes information that has implications for future realizations of earnings or stock returns. The first two explanations (incentives and selection) posit that analysts are rational; the third posits specific forms of irrational information processing.

By rational information processing, we mean that the analyst conditions forecasts, in an unbiased manner, on all publicly available information containing earnings implications. In the extreme, and setting aside other considerations momentarily, if all analysts interpreted and reported earnings forecasts in this way, we would expect to see essentially zero bias (i.e., neither optimism nor pessimism). Some analysts might unintentionally err on the high side of the subsequent earnings realization; others would err on the low side. These errors would be merely the result of uncertainty, or "noise," in the environment, however, and the errors would be consistent with other research indicating that analysts apparently have incentives to forecast accurately as a way to reduce the probability of demotion or job "turnover" (Hong and Kubik 2003; Mikhail, Walther, and Willis 1999).[18]

Because research has shown a preponderance of errors on the high side, however, the noise scenario seems unlikely; hence, more complicated

---

[18]Although Mikhail et al. (1999) documented a relationship between turnover and relative forecast accuracy, they found no relationship between forecast bias and turnover.

explanations have been advanced. Incentive and selection explanations posit that analysts "know" (in a rational sense) the future earnings outcome for a company but choose either to add upward bias to that knowledge or withhold the knowledge altogether. The final explanation we consider, the presence of a cognitive bias, allows for the possibility that the analyst may not know future earnings; that is, he or she may fail to formulate earnings expectations in an unbiased and rational manner.

Incentives. Incentive explanations for forecast optimism suggest that analysts report untruthfully—issuing larger earnings forecasts than they expect to see realized in light of the company's earnings prospects. In fact, widespread concerns about untruthful reporting motivated the passage of Regulation Analyst Certification (Reg AC), effective 14 April 2003. This law requires stock analysts (and others) who issue reports on a security to certify in their reports that the views expressed are accurate reflections of their personal (unobservable) beliefs.

A prevalent explanation for purposeful inflation of analysts' earnings forecasts is the desire of analysts to attract revenue-generating business for their employers through investment banking business or underwriting fees. Academic studies advancing this motive for unwarranted optimism typically document more favorable earnings forecasts and stock recommendations from "affiliated" analysts than from "unaffiliated" analysts for the same company. Affiliated analysts are defined as analysts employed by brokerage firms that provide, or have recently provided (over the prior one to three years), underwriting arrangements or investment banking services for the followed company. If the company managers prefer more optimistic forecasts to less optimistic forecasts, then to pursue future banking business for their employers, affiliated analysts may attempt to curry favor (both with the client managers and the analysts' employers) by issuing higher-than-warranted earnings estimates. (We discuss studies of the effect of analysts' relationships with corporate managers in Chapter 3.)

Such potential investment banking conflicts became so prevalent in the 1990s that the SEC, other regulators, and New York State Attorney General Elliot Spitzer announced on 21 December 2002 a settlement in which 10 securities firms, although neither admitting nor denying misleading investors, agreed to pay fines of $1.44 billion to, in part, resolve charges that they gave biased stock ratings to companies that were clients of their employers' banking divisions. Richard A. Grasso, then chairman and chief executive officer of the New York Stock Exchange, testifying before Congress on 7 May 2003, subsequently echoed this conflict:

...[E]ach firm encouraged an environment in which research analysts were repeatedly subject to inappropriate influence by investment bankers, and the analysts' objectivity and independence was compromised as a result of that influence. The firms' policies and procedures failed to protect research analysts from the significant investment banking influences and conflicts of interest. (p. 2)

The possibility that investment banking conflicts might color analysts' reporting behavior had already been the subject of investigations in academic research several years before the SEC settlement. Dugar and Nathan had examined whether the existence of an investment banking relationship between the analyst's employer and the client company influences the affiliated analyst's reports. Using a sample of 250 matched pairs (representing 102 companies) for the 1983–88 period, Dugar and Nathan found consistent evidence that affiliated analysts' reports are more optimistic than unaffiliated analysts' reports. In particular, the mean signed forecast error (a measure of the bias in analysts' earnings forecasts) for affiliated analyst earnings forecasts was 4.04 percent, compared with 2.80 percent for unaffiliated analysts. Using a 5-point scale to aggregate information about stock recommendations (1 = strong buy, 2 = buy, 3 = hold, 4 = sell, and 5 = strong sell), the authors showed that the average stock recommendation given by affiliated analysts was 2.24, compared with 2.49 for unaffiliated analysts. Both the difference in mean forecast errors (of 1.24 percentage points) and in mean stock recommendations (0.25 percentage points) were significant at better than the 1 percent level; hence, the probability of finding these results by chance is less than 1 in 100.

Lin and McNichols probed the role of underwriting arrangements in influencing the bias in affiliated and unaffiliated analysts' reports. For their sample of 2,400 seasoned equity offerings made in 1989–1994, they identified the lead and co-underwriters for each offering; analysts employed by these firms were defined as affiliated analysts; analysts following the same company but employed by other brokerage houses were defined as unaffiliated analysts. The authors found no evidence that affiliated analysts' earnings forecasts, either for the current year or one year ahead, exhibit greater optimism than unaffiliated analysts' forecasts (e.g., both affiliated and unaffiliated analysts demonstrated mean optimism in current-year earnings forecasts of about 7 percent of share price). A similar finding of no difference in the optimism in affiliated and unaffiliated earnings forecasts was found by Hansen and Sarin (1998). Lin and McNichols did find, however, that affiliated analysts' five-year earnings growth forecasts and stock recommendations are significantly more optimistic than those of their unaffiliated counterparts: The mean growth forecast for affiliated analysts was 21.3 percent, compared with 20.7 percent for unaffiliated analysts (with the difference significant at the 5 percent level), and the mean stock recommendation, on a 5-point scale, was 1.74 for affiliated analysts and 2.10 for unaffiliated analysts (difference significant at the 1 percent level).

Dechow, Hutton, and Sloan (2000) extended the literature on the effects of underwriting activities on analysts' reports by investigating the link between the optimism in analysts' earnings growth forecasts at the time of equity offerings. Similar to Lin and McNichols, Dechow et al. found that affiliated analysts' growth forecasts are more optimistic around the time of equity offerings than are unaffiliated analysts' forecasts. They further showed that the degree of optimism in affiliated analysts' growth forecasts increases in line with the underwriting fees paid to the affiliated analysts' employer.

Michaely and Womack (1999) also reported greater optimism in growth forecasts and stock recommendations for affiliated analysts around initial public offerings. Moreover, they showed that the stocks recommended by underwriter-affiliated analysts perform more poorly than the stocks recommended by unaffiliated analysts before, at the time of, and after the issuance of these recommendations. Thus, not only are the recommendations made by affiliated analysts themselves more optimistic, but their profitability is lower than that of the recommendations made by unaffiliated analysts.

Research points to trading commissions as an additional source of bias in analysts' reporting behavior. Hayes (1998) modeled the role that trading commissions play in determining the accuracy and availability of analysts' reports.[19] Her theoretical study showed that analysts issue more accurate reports for stocks they think will perform well (buy stocks) and less accurate reports for stocks they expect to perform poorly (sell stocks). This relationship occurs because analysts' incentives to generate trading commissions are positively related to trading volume. She showed that for buy stocks, trading volume is increased by providing more precise information (because precise information reduces the investor's perceived risk); for sell stocks, the opposite occurs.

Irvine (2000) provided empirical evidence about the relationship between trading commissions and analysts' coverage decisions. He used a unique dataset obtained from the Toronto Stock Exchange (TSE), which identifies the name of the broker(s) involved in each stock transaction of the 100 largest TSE-listed companies. Irvine used data for 1 September 1993 through 31 August 1994. For each company, Irvine linked the trading volume associated with each broker name with analysts who worked for the same broker/firm

---

[19]Although researchers have not studied the effect of brokerage incentives on forecast bias, the results reported by Hayes and by McNichols and O'Brien (1997) suggest that such incentives might induce favorable reporting of information. In particular, Hayes noted that because the pool of potential investors who can trade on a buy recommendation exceeds the pool of investors who can trade on a sell (given short-selling restrictions), all else being equal, the chance of affecting trading with a buy recommendation is greater than with a sell recommendation. This prediction is supported by results reported by McNichols and O'Brien, who showed that analysts are much more likely to initiate coverage of stocks that they expect to do well in the future.

and analysts who did not. His research design explored the relationship between trading volume and analyst reporting behavior. In particular, he predicted that brokerage volume would be higher for a stock when the brokerage house also had analysts covering that stock. He found that brokerage firms that provided analyst coverage increased their trading volume by 3.8 percent (after other factors affecting trading volume were controlled for) relative to brokerage firms that did not cover the stock.

Given the substantial evidence showing greater optimism in the reports and coverage decisions of affiliated analysts, a reasonable question is whether investors understand this bias. That is, can investors "see through" this optimism and adjust the information provided accordingly? Evidence on whether investors are able to discount the optimism in affiliated analysts' reports goes to the heart of much of the debate concerning Reg AC; this regulation implicitly assumes that at least some investors are unable to see through the behavior of affiliated analysts. But although some investors are surely fooled by affiliated analysts' bias, our interest lies more in whether the investing public, *on average*, is able to discern and correct for this bias. As we will discuss, research investigating this question has generally found that investors *do* discount the information in affiliated analysts' reports, which indicates some sophistication in the processing abilities of the marginal investor. Importantly, however, these tests cannot shed light on whether the adjustment that the average investor makes fully corrects for these biases.

Dugar and Nathan examined whether investors discount the information in affiliated analysts' reports by comparing stock market reactions with the information contained in the two types of reports. They found that the market reacts less intensely to a unit of earnings information conveyed by affiliated analysts' reports than it reacts to information in unaffiliated analysts' reports. This evidence is consistent with the market discounting the information conveyed by affiliated analysts.

Further evidence of investor understanding of affiliated analysts' biases was reported by Lin and McNichols. They showed that, although the returns to affiliated analysts' strong buy and buy recommendations are indistinguishable from the returns to similar recommendations made by unaffiliated analysts, the returns to their hold recommendations differ significantly. In particular, three-day abnormal returns following hold recommendations made by analysts employed by lead underwriters were significantly more negative than the three-day abnormal returns to hold recommendations made by unaffiliated analysts. The authors interpreted this finding as indicating that investors are more likely to view an affiliated analyst's hold recommendation as a sell recommendation.

Dechow et al. also probed the link between optimism in growth forecasts and the well-documented result that companies experience unusually low stock returns in the three to five years following equity offerings ("postoffering underperformance").[20] They found that postoffering underperformance is more pronounced for the companies that receive the highest growth forecasts by affiliated analysts. They also showed that, after the optimism in the affiliated growth forecasts was controlled for, the long-run underperformance of the offering companies disappeared. One interpretation of these results is that investors are misled by affiliated analysts' optimism at the time of the offering and that the true growth prospects of the company lead to corrections in price over the five years following the offering.

In summary, a number of incentives have been hypothesized to operate on analysts' reporting decisions. These incentives may induce analysts to report untruthfully—in effect, to misrepresent their private views in their public disclosures. The extant empirical research is consistent with the idea that institutional incentives (in the form of underwriting, investment banking, and brokerage commissions) influence analysts' reporting behavior—including their coverage decisions and their optimism—in the predicted way. Specifically, research shows that affiliated analysts issue more optimistic earnings growth forecasts and stock recommendations than their unaffiliated counterparts. Whether investors are aware of and discount this bias is an open empirical question. Although research shows that investors react less strongly to affiliated analysts' reports than unaffiliated analysts' reports (which is consistent with investors weighting the affiliated analysts' information less), current research designs have not revealed whether the degree of discounting is commensurate with the observed bias.

Selection. In contrast to incentive-based explanations for analyst forecast optimism, which posit that analysts report untruthfully, the selection bias explanation suggests that analysts report truthfully but *selectively*. That is, analysts provide truthful forecasts for companies about which they hold positive views and no forecasts for other companies (McNichols and O'Brien). Thus, selection is conjectured to alter the analyst's coverage decision by inducing the analyst to withhold information rather than convey it falsely.

---

[20]For summaries of the literature on postoffering underperformance, see Loughran and Ritter (1995) and Spiess and Affleck-Graves (1995). Also, see recent work by Brav and Gompers (1997), Brav (2000), and Brav, Geczy, and Gompers (2000), who argue that postoffering underperformance appears to be less a result of these companies being engaged in equity offerings than a result of characteristics of the companies being covered (they tend to be small and have high book-to-market ratios) and to inadequacies in the standard statistical techniques used to identify postoffering performance.

In the selection explanation, the reason for an analyst's silence is not explicitly considered. One possibility, however, is that analysts choose to remain silent rather than potentially displease company managers, or their own employers, by issuing unfavorable earnings forecasts.

From an investor's perspective, if analysts deliberately tilt their stock coverage toward securities about which they hold favorable views, the resulting distribution of analysts' earnings forecasts is incomplete relative to the entire distribution of analysts' reported *and unreported* earnings expectations. Such a distribution is referred to as "truncated," and it increases a researcher's chance of calculating an optimistic bias from observed analyst forecast errors—a bias that would not be present were the entire distribution visible to the researcher.

Evidence of such truncation was provided by McNichols and O'Brien. Using a large sample of analyst reports in the 1987–94 period, McNichols and O'Brien reported that analysts tend to initiate coverage on stocks they believe will perform well and to stop coverage on stocks they believe will perform poorly. This reporting behavior causes the distribution of stock recommendations to be highly skewed, leading to the observed pattern of a preponderance of buy recommendations. Further evidence that analysts are not merely "window-dressing" the stocks they choose to cover but actually have convictions about the stock's future superior performance comes from the subsequent realized returns on equity observed for added and dropped stocks. Specifically, McNichols and O'Brien found that added stocks have higher subsequent returns on equity than dropped stocks, which suggests that analysts' beliefs about the stock are, in fact, grounded in fundamental information.

Hayes and Levine (2000) provided evidence on the effects of selection on the distribution of analysts' forecast errors. They documented more optimism in the (observed) distribution of truncated analyst forecast errors than in the (unobserved) distribution of untruncated analyst forecast errors (the unobserved errors were estimated by using maximum-likelihood estimations). They further showed that the earnings estimates from the untruncated distribution are more accurate than the earnings estimates from the truncated distribution.

Cognitive Bias. Ideally, an analyst fully incorporates all relevant information available when making a forecast. Such information processing would be consistent with standard economic models of rational individual behavior: Information is fully exploited in an unbiased manner. Behavioral science research, however, has identified several cognitive biases that suggest analysts may not fully incorporate all available information.[21] Thus, this research suggests the antithesis of the previously discussed incentive and selection explanations. That

---

[21]See Tversky and Kahneman (1974) for an introduction to this literature, and for discussions, see, for example, *FAJ* (1999) and Shefrin (1999).

is, rather than process information *correctly* and knowingly report it *untruthfully* (or remain silent), cognitive explanations allow for the possibility that the analyst, affected by one or more cognitive biases, unknowingly processes information incorrectly but reports that (flawed) assessment truthfully.

Most prior research in this domain has concluded that analysts underreact to prior information. Analysts are said to underreact if they revise outstanding earnings forecasts or issue new forecasts that insufficiently adjust for publicly available information at the forecast release date. By "insufficient adjustment," we mean that following disclosure of bad (good) news, the analyst fails to revise a forecast downward (upward) *as far as it should be revised* given the news in the disclosure. Note that if forecasting behavior were completely rational, all publicly available information would be fully used. If analysts are affected by a cognitive "information processing" bias, the information is not used fully or correctly—thus, not rationally.

The underreaction explanation has been documented in experimental research (Affleck-Graves, Davis, and Mendenhall 1990; Cianci 2000) and in numerous empirical studies (Abarbanell and Bernard 1992; Ali, Klein, and Rosenfeld 1992; Francis and Philbrick; Jacob and Lys 1999; Klein 1990; Lys and Sohn 1990; Mendenhall 1991; Mikhail, Walther, and Willis 2003b).[22] This body of work has established that analysts underreact to recent information in earnings and stock returns by documenting a significant relationship between the news in recent disclosures and the forecast errors associated with analysts' forecasts made following those disclosures.

Section Summary. Three general classes of explanations have been advanced for optimism in analysts' reporting behavior—incentives, selection, and cognitive biases. Research testing these explanations has generally found support for each as a source of analyst bias. Note, however, that the literature has addressed each explanation separately; that is, each study focused on a single explanation: The researchers exploited a research methodology that was designed to identify biased reporting behavior if it exists and to attribute that bias to the single explanation. For example, comparisons of the properties of the reports made by affiliated and unaffiliated analysts for the same company and time period are intended to rule out other explanations for differences in those properties (such as differences in company- or time-specific factors) and to increase the likelihood that the observed effects are a result of the conditioning variable for determining affiliation status (i.e., underwriting, investment banking, or brokerage activities).

---

[22]An exception is Easterwood and Nutt (1999), who found that consensus analysts' forecasts overreact to past favorable information but underreact to past unfavorable information.

Although such research designs are powerful in detecting analyst reporting behavior associated with *each* explanation, they cannot distinguish among explanations that may be correlated. For example, institutional *incentives* may drive analysts to *select* companies they believe will have favorable performance; if so, then evidence on the selection explanation is not independent of evidence on incentive explanations. Even if the explanations are not linked by some plausible economic reasoning, they may be empirically linked; that is, analysts who are most susceptible to cognitive biases may also happen to be the most selective in choosing which stocks to cover. The danger with correlated explanations is that researchers may improperly attribute causality to one explanation when, in fact, another explanation is driving the results.

New Evidence on Forecast Optimism and Its Determinants

In this section, we report new evidence on the influences of incentive, selection, and cognitive biases in explaining analyst forecast optimism. The contribution of these analyses is their examination of these explanations *jointly* after controlling for other factors known to affect analyst forecasting behavior (such as some of the data issues described in Chapter 1). By analyzing the explanations simultaneously, we can comment on the uniqueness and relative importance of each explanation.

Sample and Variables. We examined analysts' earnings forecasts made for all companies with security price data from the Center for Research in Security Prices, Compustat financial data, and analyst forecasts of current-year EPS available in the Zacks Investment Research database for any year $t = 1980 \ldots 1996$. We required that analysts' forecasts be released after the company's announcement of year $t - 1$ earnings to ensure that prior-year financial statement data, which we used to calculate some of the independent variables, had been disclosed.

We measured the signed realized forecast error for analyst i's year t forecast for company j (adjusted for stock splits and stock dividends) as

$$Err_{i,j,t} = \frac{F_{i,j,t} - A_{j,t}}{P_{j,t-10}}, \tag{2.1}$$

where

$\quad F_{i,j,t}$ = analyst i's year t forecast for company j

$\quad A_{j,t}$ = company j's year t EPS before discontinued operations, extraordinary items, and the cumulative effects of any accounting changes

$\quad P_{j,t-10}$ = company j's share price 10 trading days before the Zacks forecast release date

Thus, *Err* measures how much the analyst's forecast of annual earnings differs from the earnings number, as a percentage of share price, reported by the company at its subsequent annual earnings announcement. Note that for analyses reported in this section, optimism is indicated by *positive* values of *Err*; pessimism is indicated by *negative* values of *Err*.

Because one of our explanations for analyst optimism (selection) operates on the *existence* of analysts' forecasts, it was crucial that our sample also capture the truncated portion of the forecast-error distribution. For this purpose, we expanded the sample to include companies with financial data but *without* analysts' forecasts in Zacks; we coded these 349,172 "Not Followed" observations as *Err* = missing. Thus, we assumed that companies without analyst forecasts in Zacks were not covered; violations of this assumption would weaken our tests but not bias them.

▓ *Incentives variables.* We included two variables to capture incentive explanations for optimism. First, we measured analysts' incentives to issue biased reports to induce greater trading volume as the logarithm of company j's average monthly shares traded over the 12 months ending the month preceding the forecast release date, $Vol_{j,t}$. For the $Err_{i,j,t}$ = missing observations, $Vol_{j,t}$ was measured as the logarithm of company j's average monthly shares traded during the calendar year. We measured *Vol* with a logarithmic transformation because this transformation improves the fit of our estimated models to the observed data.

Second, to measure analysts' incentives to issue biased reports to secure or maintain client banking relationships, we gathered data on whether the analyst issuing an earnings forecast worked for a brokerage house that served as lead or co-underwriter on any of the company's debt or equity issuances in the current or previous two years. We used an indicator variable, $UW_{i,j,t}$ =1 if analyst i's employer was a lead or co-underwriter of any of company j's debt and equity issuances in years $t - 2$, $t - 1$, or t. For the $Err_{i,j,t}$ = missing observations, $UW_{i,j,t}$ = 0.

▓ *Selection variables.* Our test of selection was predicated on subsequent company performance being inversely related to forecast errors: Companies with poor future prospects are less likely to induce analyst reporting, which implies that the observed distribution of (realized) forecast errors is truncated from below. This truncation leads to the prediction that companies with poor prospects have more optimistic forecast errors than do companies with good prospects. Following McNichols and O'Brien, to proxy for the subsequent performance of company j, we used the realized industry-adjusted return on equity of company j in year $t + 1$, $IROE_{j,t+1}$; we calculated it as company j's realized return on equity in year $t + 1$ less the median realized return on equity for all companies in the same two-digit SIC as company j in year $t + 1$. We industry-adjusted the return on equity measure for each company because financial ratios are well known to vary among industries and through time. Industry adjustment, therefore, allows more meaningful comparisons of future performance for companies in different industries and at different points in time. We expected *IROE* to be inversely related to the extent of optimism in analysts' forecasts.

      Cognitive bias variables. We used the company's prior-year stock return, $Ret_{j,t-1}$, to proxy for analyst underreaction to recent information about company performance. We obtained similar results if we replace $Ret_{j,t-1}$ by the company's most recently announced earnings surprise as the measure of prior performance.

      Company-specific variables. Evidence documented in prior work (Brown 2001; Hwang, Jan, and Basu 1996) showed that analysts' earnings forecasts are significantly more optimistic for companies that reported a loss in the year of the forecast. Therefore, we included $Loss_{j,t} = 1$ if company j had a loss in year t; otherwise, $Loss_{j,t} = 0$.

We also included a variable for size (measured by the log of company j's total assets at the end of year $t-1$, $Assets_{j,t-1}$) because prior research has shown that analysts' forecasts are less optimistic for the larger companies (Das, Levine, and Sivaramakrishnan 1998; Lim 2001).

Finally, we included the age of the forecast because prior research has shown that optimism in analysts' annual forecasts decreases as forecast age decreases (O'Brien; Richardson, Teoh, and Wysocki, forthcoming 2004). That is, analyst forecasts become less optimistic as the earnings announcement date draws near. We measured forecast age, *Age*, as the number of calendar days between the annual earnings announcement and the forecast release date.

Main Tests and Results. Our empirical tests examined the marginal ability of each explanation for optimism to explain the distribution of forecast errors, where that distribution was augmented by companies on which analysts did not report. Because all sample observations did not have numeric values for *Err* (that is, *Err* = missing, not zero for Not Followed companies), we could not use standard statistical procedures (such as ordinary least-squares or truncated least-squares methods) to estimate the relationship between *Err* and the independent variables. Setting *Err* = 0 for the $Err_{i,j,t}$ = missing observations also was not appropriate because (1) tests of selection require that *missing* observations be importantly distinct from *unbiased* forecasted observations and (2) arbitrarily setting *Err* = 0 for observations in which $F_{i,j,t}$ did not exist implicitly (and inappropriately) ranked missing forecasts as more optimistic than pessimistic forecasts.

To address these estimation issues, we grouped forecasts into three discrete categories, $ErrCat_{i,j,t}$:

$ErrCat_{i,j,t} = 1$ if $Err_{i,j,t} > 0$ (analyst i's forecast for company j was *optimistic*).

$ErrCat_{i,j,t} = 2$ if $Err_{i,j,t}$ = missing (there was no analyst forecast because company j was Not Followed).

$ErrCat_{i,j,t} = 3$ if $Err_{i,j,t} \leq 0$ (i.e., analyst i's forecast for company j was zero or pessimistic). We refer to this group as *pessimistic*. Our results were not sensitive to excluding forecast errors that were zero from the pessimistic category.

The disadvantage of this grouping is that we lost information on the magnitude, but not the sign, of the realized forecast error; the advantage is that we retained information about whether the company was followed or not.

We examined the relationship between the test variables and the control variables and the likelihood of a given observation being classified as $ErrCat$ = 1, 2, or 3. Because the results of the more complex multinomial estimation procedure are similar to the results of estimating two binary logit models, we report only the logit model results:[23]

$$\Pr[ErrCat_{i,j,t} = (1,3)] = \mathrm{logit}(d_{0,t} + d_{1,t}Age_{i,j,t} + d_{2,t}Assets_{j,t-1}$$
$$+ d_{3,t}Loss_{j,t} + d_{4,t}IROE_{j,t+1} + d_{5,t}Ret_{j,t-1} \qquad (2.2)$$
$$+ d_{6,t}UW_{i,j,t} + d_{7,t}Vol_{j,t})$$

$$\Pr[ErrCat_{i,j,t} = (2,3)] = \mathrm{logit}(d_{0,t} + d_{1,t}Assets_{j,t-1} + d_{2,t}Loss_{j,t}$$
$$+ d_{3,t}IROE_{j,t+1} + d_{4,t}Ret_{j,t-1} + d_{5,t}UW_{i,j,t} \qquad (2.3)$$
$$+ d_{6,t}Vol_{j,t}).$$

The models given by Equations 2.2 and 2.3 use pessimistic forecasts ($ErrCat_{i,j,t}$ = 3) as the benchmark because, implicitly, this approach is what most prior studies did when they examined a continuous forecast-error metric, such as Err, which takes on positive (optimistic) and negative (pessimistic)

---

[23]Begg and Gray (1984) showed that estimating separate binary logit models, rather than a single multinomial model, results in slightly less efficient coefficient estimates. This loss of efficiency worked against our finding statistically significant results.

values.[24] Intuitively, estimation of the model in Equation 2.2 reveals whether, and by how much, a one unit change in each of the right-hand variables affects the likelihood that the analyst will report an optimistic forecast rather than a pessimistic forecast. Estimation of the model in Equation 2.3 reveals whether, and by how much, a one unit change in each of the right-hand variables affects the likelihood of the analyst reporting no forecast at all rather than a pessimistic forecast. We estimated Equation 2.2 and 2.3 for each year and then averaged the coefficient estimates across years.

The results are shown in **Table 2.1**. We report the predicted sign of the coefficient (in brackets), the *p*-values for the statistical significance of the mean value of the coefficient, and the number of years (out of 17 years for which we had data) that the coefficient was of the predicted sign.

Table 2.1. Results of Tests for Likelihood of Optimistic Forecast and Likelihood of No Forecast

Model	Age	Assets	Loss	IROE	Ret	UW	Vol
Equation 2.2:							
Pr[*ErrCat* = (1, 3)]	+0.0025	–0.0403	ı1.8054	–1.1178	–0.5493	–0.0502	+0.0850
Predicted sign	[+]	[–]	[+]	[–]	[–]	[+]	[+]
p-Value	0.01	0.01	0.01	0.01	0.01	0.15	0.01
Years	17	10	17	15	17	9	14
Equation 2.3:							
Pr[*ErrCat* = (2, 3)]		–0.2175	+2.1033	–0.2581	–0.6403	–15.1190	–0.6406
Predicted sign		[–]	[+]	[–]	[–]	[+]	[–]
p-Value		0.01	0.01	0.02	0.01	0.01	0.01
Years		16	17	12	15	0	17

In terms of the control variables (*Age*, *Assets*, and *Loss*), the Table 2.1 results are consistent with prior research in showing that older forecasts, forecasts associated with loss observations, and forecasts made for small companies are more likely to be optimistic.

Turning to the variables capturing the three explanations for optimism, we focus, first, on the selection explanation, which pertains to the coefficient on *IROE*. The results for Equation 2.2 in Table 2.1 show that analysts' forecasts are less optimistic for companies with better subsequent performance and (for Equation 2.3) that analysts are more likely to withhold forecasts for the

[24]We excluded *Age* from Equation 2.2 because it takes on missing values for all Not Followed observations (i.e., $ErrCat_{i,j,t} = 2$). When we set *Age* equal to the mean or median sample forecast age and estimated Equation 2.2 with *Age* included, we were able to draw similar inferences to those reported.

companies with poorer prospects. Both results are highly statistically significant (at the 1 percent and 2 percent levels, respectively), and both results were observed in a majority of years (15 and 12, respectively). These findings are consistent with the selection explanation for optimism, which holds that (1) analyst forecasts are less optimistic for companies with better subsequent performance and (2) analysts are more likely to withhold forecasts for companies with less promising prospects.

Turning to the cognitive variable capturing underreaction (the company's past stock return, *Ret*), we found a significant negative association between *Err* and *Ret*. This finding, which is significant in both equations and was observed for most sample years, is consistent with prior studies' findings of analyst underreaction: The larger (smaller) the prior returns, the less (more) likely that the analyst's forecast will be optimistic. This finding is also consistent with analysts failing to incorporate all publicly available and relevant earnings-related information at the time they release their forecasts.

As for the incentive explanations, note that Table 2.1 shows the mean coefficient on *Vol* in Equation 2.2 to be positive, meaning that analysts are more likely to issue optimistic forecasts (versus pessimistic forecasts) for companies whose securities offer greater opportunities for trading commissions, which is consistent with our expectation. The results for Equation 2.3 given in Table 2.1 show that, faced with a decision about whether to issue a pessimistic report or not to issue a report, greater trading volume decreases the likelihood of not issuing a report. That is, greater trading volume is more likely to result in the analyst issuing a pessimistic forecast than issuing no forecast at all. Both of these findings are highly statistically significant (at the 1 percent level) and were observed consistently across the individual years composing the sample. They are consistent with the prediction that incentives associated with brokerage commissions encourage forecasting activity that increases trading volume.

Finally, the results show little evidence that underwriting activities (*UW*) are likely to lead to more optimistic forecast reporting. In particular, Table 2.1 contains no evidence (i.e., insignificant coefficient estimates on the incentive variables) from Equation 2.2 that the existence of underwriting arrangements leads to greater optimism in current-year earnings forecasts (which is consistent with results reported by Hansen and Sarin and by Lin and McNichols). Moreover, the results for Equation 2.3 for *UW* reveal negative coefficient estimates (not positive estimates as predicted by an incentive explanation). These negative values suggest that affiliated analysts are *more* likely to issue a pessimistic forecast for a company where their employer has been a recent underwriter than to not issue a forecast for such companies.

As a check on the results, we also estimated a simple ordinary least-squares regression of the forecast error on the set of seven independent variables. Because only followed companies have numerical values of *Err*, this regression allowed us to comment only on whether and how the various explanations for optimism affect the forecasting activity of followed companies. The results are in **Table 2.2**.

Table 2.2. Ordinary Least-Squares Regression of *Err* on Seven Variables

Statistic	*Age*	*Assets*	*Loss*	*IROE*	*Ret*	*UW*	*Vol*
Coefficient	+0.0020	–0.0246	+0.9392	–0.5699	–0.4674	–0.0379	+0.0598
Predicted sign	[+]	[–]	[+]	[–]	[–]	[+]	[+]
p-Value	0.01	0.04	0.01	0.01	0.01	0.17	0.01
Years	17	9	17	14	17	2	14

The signs and significance of the coefficient estimates in Table 2.2 are similar in all respects to the inferences drawn from the results for Equation 2.2. That is, we found more forecast optimism for companies with poor subsequent performance (as proxied by future industry-adjusted return on equity, *IROE*), with poorer past performance (as captured by past stock returns, *Ret*), and with greater trading volume (*Vol*). We found no reliable association between forecast optimism and whether the analyst's employer had an underwriting relationship with the company.

Section Summary. Overall, the results of our analyses indicate that variables capturing incentive, selection, and cognitive factors explain analyst forecast errors, are incremental to each other, and are incremental to the effects of forecast age, company size, and whether the company incurred a loss in the forecast year. That is, our tests indicate that each of these explanations is distinct from the others and contributes meaningfully to explaining forecast optimism.

We conclude the following. First, analysts' forecasting behavior is consistent with their strategically tilting coverage toward companies with better earnings prospects and away from companies with worse prospects, which is consistent with selection. Second, analysts exhibit underreaction: They fail to incorporate all publicly available earnings-related information at the time of a forecast release. And finally, trading volume appears to affect analysts' forecasting behavior whereas prior underwriting business does not.

Have Factors Changed over Time?

In the tests of the influence of three explanations for analyst optimism that were described in the previous section, we used each year in our sample period as the unit of analysis and then averaged the results across the 17 years of our full sample period. The interesting question that we explore in this section is whether any changes have occurred during the period in whether and how these factors explain analysts' forecast errors. For example, a finding that analysts' forecast errors are explained less today by incentives than they were 20 years ago would suggest that analysts have become more independent of their employers over time.

Our analyses here are exploratory because theory and previous research provide little basis for forming expectations about trends in the intensity of selection, incentive, and cognitive explanations. Several observations, however, suggest a decrease in the impact of these variables on forecast errors during our sample period.

First, the data suggest that analysts may be ranging more widely than in the past in selecting companies to follow. Although both the number of securities and the number of publicly traded companies increased over our sample period, the number of analysts increased at a faster rate. We calculated that the number of security analysts increased at an annualized growth rate of 10.2 percent between 1980 and 1996 whereas the annualized growth rate for public companies was 3.4 percent. The percentage of companies followed by at least one analyst increased from 26 percent in 1980 to 66 percent in 1996. If some of the increase in the population of analysts has gone to covering companies not previously followed, these calculations suggest that analyst self-selection may be less intense in more recent time periods.

Second, although numerous studies have documented that analysts underreact to prior stock returns and prior earnings, recent work by Mikhail et al. (2003b) indicates that the more-experienced analysts exhibit less underreaction. Their finding that this cognitive bias is attenuated in some analysts over time suggests that we may observe declines in the extent of analyst underreaction *if* average analyst experience increased over the sample period. Average analyst experience might have increased or decreased, depending on, among other things, expansion or contraction of the research industry and entry and exit patterns of analysts from the industry and from forecast databases.

To explore this issue, we calculated the experience of each analyst who made at least one forecast during our sample period; our measure of experience was the number of prior quarterly earnings forecasts made by the analyst for the same company. Such a "task-based" measure of forecasting experience is usually preferred to a "time-based" measure of experience, such as the number of years or quarters that an analyst has followed a particular company.

A task-based measure of experience is designed to capture the extent to which an analyst has performed the forecasting activity for a particular company and, therefore, captures the analyst's familiarity with the company's earnings process (see Mikhail et al. 1997, 2003a for a discussion).[25] **Figure 2.1** shows the change in the mean of the company-specific measure of analyst experience over the 1980–96 period.

The mean experience level at the beginning of 1996 indicates that the average analyst had about 10 prior quarters of company-specific forecasting experience (as determined since the inception of the Zacks database in 1980).[26]

Figure 2.1.   Trend in Analyst Company-Specific Experience, 1980–96

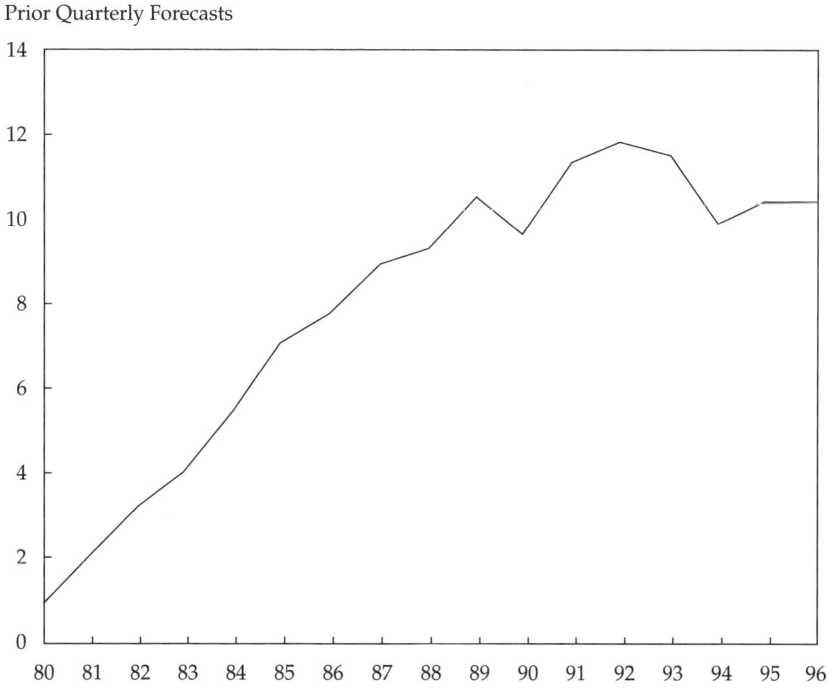

Prior Quarterly Forecasts

[25]Alternatives to measures of company-specific experience are (1) industry-specific experience (the number of prior quarters for which the analyst issued an earnings forecast for any company in the same industry) and (2) general experience (the number of prior quarters for which the analyst issued any earnings forecasts). These measures are highly correlated with company-specific experience (see Mikhail et al. 1997).

[26]Tests of trends in the mean and the median values revealed a significant increase in analyst experience over the period, even when we excluded the early sample years (1980–1985)—a period when, by construction, we expected the number of prior forecast quarters to increase (because the Zacks data do not begin until 1980).

Casual empiricism and statistical analysis show a clear upward trend in the amount of experience possessed by analysts. Given this change, we predict that the extent of underreaction declined during our sample period.

Finally, given the greater incidence of shareholder litigation over misleading, and almost always optimistic, company disclosures in recent times, we expected corporate management to be more likely to temper analysts' forecasts when the forecasts were overly optimistic in the recent period. Specifically, although securities laws do not require corporate managers to correct overly optimistic information that they did not provide, the laws do hold managers liable for forecasts, or commentaries about analysts' or others' forecasts, that management supplied or explicitly guided. We conjectured that management is more likely to temper analysts' forecasts when analysts have incentives to be optimistic, as proxied by situations containing potential brokerage or underwriting gains to the analyst's employer. This litigation argument suggests that over time, the intensity of overoptimism associated with the brokerage and underwriting incentive explanations should decline.

To garner evidence about trends in the intensity of all the explanations for overoptimism, we regressed the series of 17 coefficient estimates obtained from the annual estimations of Equations 2.2 and 2.3 on a trend variable, which took the value of 1 in 1980 and went up to 17 by 1996. We found, consistent with the conjecture that the relatively larger growth in the analyst population versus traded companies has led to less selection bias, that the trend in the coefficient on *IROE* has been generally positive. Because evidence of selection was indicated by a negative coefficient on *IROE*, a positive trend in this coefficient means that, over time, selection has weakened as an explanation for optimism.

We found a change in the intensity of analysts' underreaction to new information by examining the trend coefficient on *Ret*. The trend coefficient for *Ret* was positive; because underreaction was evidenced by a negative coefficient on *Ret*, this result means that analyst underreaction became less severe over the sample period. This result is consistent with the increased experience of the sample analysts shown in Figure 2.1 and with Mikhail et al.'s (2003b) finding that analysts appear to learn over time about their forecast errors and partially adjust for these errors in subsequent forecasts.

Changes in the intensity of incentive explanations for optimism over time indicate that both underwriting- and commission-related incentives appear to have declined over the 1980–96 period. In particular, an unambiguous decline occurred in the intensity with which underwriting incentives affected the decision to withhold a forecast rather than issue a pessimistic one. This finding is consistent with a declining influence of underwriting activity on analyst reporting behavior. We also found that analysts became more likely to with-hold a forecast for a company with large trading volume rather than issue a pessimistic forecast for this company. Given that any type of report (favorable or unfavorable) is expected to generate more trading volume than no report, this last finding is consistent with a decreased intensity of incentives stemming from a desire to generate brokerage commissions.

Summary and Conclusions

The major explanations for analyst forecast optimism are institutional incentives stemming from the revenue-generating activities of the analyst's employer, selection on the part of analysts in choosing companies with favorable future prospects, and a common cognitive processing bias. In reviewing the empirical evidence attesting to the strength of each explanation, we found that research has generally documented that analyst reporting activity—including coverage decisions and the components of the typical analyst's report (earnings forecast, stock recommendation, growth forecast)—are affected by each of these explanations in the predicted ways. That is, analysts' reports tend to be more optimistic when (1) the analyst's firm engages in investment banking, underwriting, and/or brokerage activities involving the followed company; (2) the analyst is personally optimistic about the followed company's future performance; or (3) the analyst underreacts to recent performance signals.

Prior research has shown that these effects exist separately, and we presented new evidence that the effects also exist jointly—that is, conditional on the others—except that the effect of underwriting is less influential when other explanations are considered.

We also report new insights into whether the intensity of these explanations for analyst optimism has changed over time. We found some evidence of mitigation in the intensity of all three explanations, which we interpret as suggesting that the link between analysts' reporting behavior and these factors, or dependence of behavior on the factors, has declined over time. In the case of the institutional incentives, for example, this reduction means that over the 1980–96 period, analysts' forecasts became more independent of their employers' interests.

3. Analyst Independence from Corporate Management

One of the most common criticisms of security analysts' reports is that they rarely contain negative information. In addition to institutional incentives (in the form of investment banking, underwriting, and brokerage fees) to issue favorable reports, many claim that analysts' reliance on the companies they follow for information and earnings guidance encourages analysts to issue favorable reports—perhaps so as not to damage the analysts' ties with corporate managers. This "management relations" theory assumes (1) that managers possess information that is valuable to analysts, (2) that analysts would not be able to access this information in the absence of close communications with management, and (3) that both company managers and analysts benefit from the guidance that management provides to analysts.

In the first part of this chapter, we probe the assumptions and implications of the management relations theory. Our goal is to shed light on its perceived existence (i.e., do analysts and other market participants behave as if it exists?) and its reality (i.e., is analyst forecasting behavior consistent with a desire to cultivate relationships with management?). The results of survey research and empirical archival studies suggest that the answer to both questions is yes. The research provides no evidence, however, that analysts merely repeat what managers tell them.

The second part of this chapter examines recent regulation—in particular, Regulation Fair Disclosure (Reg FD)—that eliminates private communications between corporate managers and selected market participants. Reg FD grew out of the U.S. Securities and Exchange Commission's (SEC's) concern that some issuers of securities engage in material, nonpublic communications with certain persons (allegedly, securities analysts and/or institutional investors) before disclosing the same information publicly. The SEC's enactment of this regulation in October 2000 provides a natural sample period for examining the role that private communications between managers and analysts played before Reg FD in analysts' forecasting behavior and how that role (and now the absence of that role) affected the informational efficiency of stock markets.

We conclude with an attempt to link and synthesize the results from the first two sections and to draw inferences about the symbiotic relationship between corporate managers and securities analysts.

©2004, The Research Foundation of CFA Institute

Dependence on Management-Provided Information

The earliest study of the relationship between securities analysts and client company managers is that of Francis and Philbrick (1993), who examined whether analysts have incentives to issue favorable earnings forecasts to cultivate (or maintain) good relationships with company managers. Their study exploited two unique features of data contained in the Value Line analysts' reports. First, because Value Line performs no underwriting, investment banking, or brokerage functions, none of the typical incentives associated with these features of the analysts' employer can explain any bias in Value Line analysts' forecasts.[27] Second, although the *Value Line Investment Survey* reports contain a stock recommendation (in the form of a timeliness rank), that stock recommendation is not generated by the analyst who prepared the earnings forecast.[28] Rather, the timeliness ranks are generated independently and are, essentially, exogenous to the analyst's report. This last feature is critical to Francis and Philbrick's hypothesis, which asserts that if unfavorable timeliness ranks lead to greater deterioration of management relationships than do favorable timeliness ranks, Value Line analysts will attempt to mitigate this deterioration by providing more optimistic earnings forecasts for companies that have been assigned unfavorable timeliness ranks.

Defining the bias in Value Line analysts' forecasts as the signed forecast error (calculated in the same manner as described in Chapter 1), Francis and Philbrick found that Value Line reports containing sell recommendations (that is, those containing timeliness ranks of 4 or 5) have more negative forecast errors—indicating more optimistic forecasts—than reports containing hold recommendations (timeliness rank of 3) or buy recommendations (timeliness ranks of 1 or 2). Indeed, the relationship between the amount of optimism in the earnings forecast and the unfavorableness of the stock recommendation in their sample period (1987–1989) is monotonic. Moreover, the increasing pattern of optimism from buy to hold to sell recommendations was observed for all forecast-error metrics—unscaled, scaled by the absolute value of the forecasted earnings per share (EPS) forecast, and scaled by share price.

[27] See Chapter 1 for a detailed description of Value Line data.

[28] Value Line's timeliness ranks place companies in one of five categories based on a proprietary combination of three criteria—nonparametric value position (a function of the company's relative price and earnings performance over the past 10 years), earnings surprise (the most recent difference between forecasted and actual quarterly earnings), and earnings momentum (the most recent difference between reported quarterly earnings and earnings for the same quarter four quarters ago). Based on these factors, Value Line creates a score for each of the 1,700 companies followed. The top 100 stocks ranked on this score are given a timeliness rank of 1 (best price performers); the next 300 receive a timeliness rank of 2 (above-average price performers); the middle 900, a rank of 3 (average price performers); the next 300, a rank of 4 (below-average price performers); and the bottom 100, a timeliness rank of 5 (worst price performers).

Francis and Philbrick interpreted the finding that Value Line analysts issue optimistic forecasts when their reports contain unfavorable recommendations as suggesting that Value Line analysts have greater incentives to placate corporate managers (by issuing favorable earnings forecasts) when they are forced to report unfavorable stock news. In further tests, the authors showed that the relationship between bias in earnings forecasts and stock recommendations is not a result of behavioral biases known to affect security analyst reporting behavior (such as underreaction, recency, and anchoring and adjustment).[29]

Eames, Glover, and Kennedy (2002) extended these analyses by investigating the relationship between earnings forecasts and stock recommendations issued by sell-side analysts as reported in the Zacks Investment Research database. Two important features of the Zacks data are (1) that most of the analysts' employers also perform other functions, including providing investment banking, underwriting, and brokerage services to their clients, and (2) that the analyst generates both the earnings forecast and the stock recommendation. So, unlike Value Line data, the stock recommendation is not exogenously included in the analyst's report.

These distinctions are important for interpreting tests of the bias in analysts' earnings forecasts conditional on stock recommendations. In the case of institutional incentives facing analysts, factors other than a desire to cultivate management relationships may influence analysts to issue optimistic forecasts. In the case of endogenous stock recommendations, the analyst now has two mechanisms by which to influence managers and the market—earnings forecasts and stock recommendations. In this situation, the analyst might bias either or both signals to cultivate management relationships. As a result, and unlike the Value Line setting, researchers have no strong a priori reason for expecting that an analyst will issue more optimistic earnings forecasts when she or he also issues a more unfavorable stock recommendation.

For a sample of about 35,000 earnings forecasts made for stocks in the 1988–96 period by analysts employed by brokers for which the annual recommendations were also known, Eames et al. found that the amount of optimism in the analyst's forecast increased with the unfavorableness of the analyst's stock recommendation. The authors showed, however, that this relationship reversed when they controlled for the level of reported earnings. That is, conditional on the earnings number reported by the company, less favorable stock recommendations were associated with less optimistic forecasts.

---

[29]Recency is the tendency of decision makers to place too much weight on recent observations. Anchoring and adjustment refer to decision makers' tendencies to adjust their judgments insufficiently for new information and, instead, to weight old information (contained in a base or benchmark) too heavily.

In a third study of the management relations hypothesis, Das, Levine, and Sivaramakrishnan (1998) exploited differences in the variability of companies' past earnings streams to develop predictions about when close ties with management are more (or less) valuable to the analyst. The authors argued that analysts have a greater need for private communications with the managers of companies whose earnings are difficult to predict. They tested this hypothesis by investigating whether companies with less-predictable earnings streams have more-optimistic earnings forecasts than companies with more-predictable earnings streams. Das et al. measured earnings predictability in three ways: (1) the past time-series variability of EPS, (2) the past time series of EPS and market returns, and (3) Value Line "earnings predictability" ranks.[30] Their results, which are robust across these three measures, are consistent with their hypothesis that companies with less-predictable earnings streams have more-optimistic earnings forecasts.

These previous studies provide indirect evidence about analysts' incentives to issue favorable earnings forecasts to curry favor with managers of the companies they follow. Presumably, the reason analysts are willing to engage in such behavior—even though it reduces the accuracy of their current forecasts—is that better management relationships improve the accuracy of analysts' *future* forecasts. That is, analysts are willing to trade off some forecast accuracy today to be privy to information tomorrow that will improve future forecast accuracy. Consistent with this argument, Laderman (1998) wrote:

> They [analysts] shy from saying things that might anger a company's managers, fearing loss of access to executives, company meetings and earnings "guidance" chats—*critical to making profit forecasts*. [Emphasis added.]

Embedded in this argument are two assumptions: (1) client managers will cut an analyst's access to management if the analyst issues unfavorable information about the company and (2) analysts benefit from communications with managers. We analyzed the research investigating each of these assumptions.

A plentitude of anecdotal evidence supports the perception that the first assumption—that analysts fear reprisals from managers if they issue negative reports—is true:[31]

---

[30]The Value Line earnings predictability index is company specific and ranges from 5 (unpredictable) to 100 (predictable). The index captures Value Line analysts' assessments of the difficulty of predicting a company's earnings.

[31]Analysts may also fear reprisals from major clients who may hold positions in stocks opposite to the analyst's true beliefs. As an example, Laderman reported a situation in which an analyst did not disclose his bearish beliefs about Boston Chicken because of fears that a mutual fund owning a substantial position in the stock would "come crashing down on him."

- A particularly salient incident of this possibility occurred after BB&T Capital Markets analyst Heather Jones downgraded Fresh Del Monte Produce. Transcripts from a February 2003 conference call with the company indicate she was barred from asking questions of company managers during the call. "Let me tell you, Heather, one thing please. You are covering us without our will, and we would not like you to ask questions on this conference call, if you may," Del Monte's chief executive officer, Mohammad Abu-Ghazaleh, responded to a question she posed (Solomon and Frank 2003).

- "It's a life among Wall Street securities analysts: Bash a company in a research report and brace for the deep freeze. . . . The retribution for negative reports takes many forms. Analysts are excluded from meetings, outings and conference calls with top company executives. . . . In some cases, offended companies try to get them [analysts writing negative earnings reports] fired" (Siconolfi 1995).

- "The great fear of the analyst when he or she goes calling on a company is finding the door shut" (Laderman).

Analyst fears of reprisal for issuing negative reports appear justified. According to a survey by Tempest Consultants sponsored by Reuters Holdings PLC (and described by Laderman), when asked how they would respond if an analyst issued a sell recommendation on their company, about one-third of company managers responded that they would not include the analyst's employer in future investment banking business and would reduce communications with the analyst and the analyst's access to management.

By eliminating an analyst from company events or failing to return or respond to the analyst's questions, company managers may effectively pressure analysts to drop coverage or change their views. Such threats have become sufficiently pervasive that in April 2003, the SEC contacted the New York Stock Exchange, NASDAQ, and the American Stock Exchange to ask them to consider establishing rules to prevent companies from exerting pressure on analysts.

Huang, Willis, and Zang (2004), however, found empirical evidence that conflicts with the anecdotal and survey evidence suggesting that managers punish analysts who issue negative reports about their companies. These authors analyzed whether analysts who issue significantly unfavorable reports about a company in the current period experience a loss in information about this company in a subsequent period; for simplicity, such analysts were referred to as "affected analysts." They proxied for information loss in three ways: (1) as a decline in forecast frequency for this company (that is, greater information loss was expected to result in affected analysts issuing fewer subsequent forecast revisions than unaffected analysts), (2) as a decline in the accuracy of affected analysts' forecasts for this company, and (3) as a decrease in the frequency of affected analysts' forecasts for this company that conveyed substantial new information. Based on a sample of more than 500,000 forecasts issued by about 30,000 analyst–company pairings in 1985–1997, they found that unfavorably affected analysts have increased accuracy in subsequent periods; they also found that the accuracy of favorably affected analysts worsened in subsequent periods.

Evidence is abundant for the second assumption—that communications with managers are valuable to analysts. For example, in surveys of key sources of information for sell-side analysts and professional investors, company management has been ranked as one of the most important sources of information (FERF 1987).

Indirect evidence that management communications with securities analysts are beneficial to analysts is also provided by the SEC's legislation of Reg FD. An important aim of this regulation was to bar management communications of material information only to selected market participants, such as securities analysts. Presumably, the SEC believed that analysts were themselves benefiting from these communications or were benefiting indirectly by passing this information on to other investors who profited.

Reg FD was aimed at curtailing *private* communications between managers and analysts (and other favored market participants), but another issue is whether *public* disclosures by managers are valuable to analysts. That is, do analysts respond to management disclosures, and does their response suggest they "parrot" what managers say or do they process the information further? Research examining whether and how analysts react to management-provided public disclosures is important because it provides empirical evidence on the extent to which analysts rely on management for new information.

In perhaps the most direct test of analysts' reliance on management-provided information, Cotter, Tuna, and Wysocki (forthcoming 2004) investigated securities analysts' responsiveness to explicit earnings guidance provided by management in the form of earnings forecasts. They found that analysts react quickly to the new information provided by management, as evidenced by a heightened frequency of earnings forecast revisions in response to management forecasts. In particular, they found that the incidence of a forecast revision the day after a management forecast is about 17 times higher than that for a forecast revision the day before the management forecast announcement. This finding suggests that the majority of analyst forecasting activity responds to earnings guidance that is publicly disclosed rather than to guidance that is not. Furthermore, the revisions made by analysts in response to management forecasts do not merely repeat what management said; rather, the authors found that analysts process the management-provided information and attempt to remove bias introduced by management.[32]

The finding that analysts respond to and use information conveyed by management forecasts of earnings is not surprising. We would expect company managers to have access to private information about the company's earnings that, when announced, would lead market participants to revise their expectations of earnings. What is interesting about the Cotter et al. results is that so much of analysts' forecasting activity appears to occur in response to public disclosures. In particular, they reported that in their 1993–2001 sample period, about 75 percent of all analyst forecasting activity occurred in the three days following quarterly earnings announcements and management earnings forecasts. Given that the preponderance of analyst activity occurs around the time of these public disclosures, this finding suggests that any private communications between managers and analysts (which may have occurred prior to Reg FD) may not be as informative as supporters of Reg FD would lead one to believe.

Effects of Reg FD

Reg FD, which the SEC implemented on 23 October 2000, prohibits companies from privately communicating material information to selected market participants without simultaneous public disclosure of the information.[33] The public disclosure must be made as soon as practical but no later than 24 hours after the initial disclosure. The intent of Reg FD, at least according to regulators, is to eliminate favored access to information that might create a nonlevel playing field among investors and lead to superior trading opportunities for selected market participants.

---

[32]For their sample of management forecasts, Cotter et al. found that managers' reports tend to contain bad news, which is consistent with managers attempting to "walk down" the market expectation of earnings. They interpreted this result as suggesting that managers wish to guide analysts to forecasting an earnings target that the company will be able to meet or beat. The importance of being able to meet or beat earnings targets (consensus earnings forecasts, last year's earnings, etc.) has been documented by several studies, notably Barth, Elliott, and Finn (1999) and Kasznik and McNichols (2002), who showed that companies with patterns of increasing earnings and patterns of meeting or exceeding analysts' earnings forecasts have higher price/earnings multiples.

[33]The first Reg FD activities undertaken by the SEC were announced on 25 November 2002. These actions consisted of three settled enforcement actions (against Raytheon Company, Secure Computing, and Siebel Systems) and one Report of Investigation (against Motorola). These activities are discussed in detail in the SEC's Press Release No. 2002-169, available at www.sec.gov.

Proponents of Reg FD claimed that the new regulation would improve the flow of information to financial markets by reducing, if not eliminating, analysts' reliance on management-provided information and by increasing the amount and quality of independent research performed by securities analysts. Moreover, by reducing reliance on management-provided information, corporate managers would have little leverage to pressure analysts to provide favorable reports to maintain or increase their access to management. Because Reg FD would reduce incentives to issue favorable reports, proponents further argued, the accuracy of analyst reports would increase after Reg FD.

Opponents of Reg FD countered these claims by arguing that Reg FD would have a "chilling effect" on corporate disclosure; rather than increasing the amount of management-provided information, Reg FD would reduce such information. Reduced disclosures were expected for two reasons. First, managers would be reluctant to communicate complex information in public disclosures without analysts being forewarned so as to provide guidance and context for interpreting the information. Second, managers would be reluctant to disclose any information solely to analysts (and institutional investors) in the wake of Reg FD because of concerns about the rules and enforcement of the regulation. In addition to reducing the amount of information, opponents argued, Reg FD would also change the timing of corporate disclosures. In particular, Reg FD would replace the continuous information flows between companies and analysts with discrete information flows related to management-provided public disclosure.

For these reasons, opponents argued that Reg FD would not only not have the intended effects claimed by regulators (of improved information flow and increased accuracy of information) but also would probably result in deterioration in informational efficiency and accuracy. Such deterioration would affect direct measures of the amount and quality of information conveyed (by analysts and by company managers) and indirect measures of informational efficiency, such as the volatility of stock returns. Specifically, critics argued that stock return volatility would increase rather than decrease after Reg FD.

Not surprisingly, the security analyst industry largely opposed Reg FD. Survey evidence reported by the Securities Industry Association (SIA 2001) and the Association for Investment Management and Research (now, CFA Institute; see AIMR 2001) indicated that the majority of securities analysts believed that Reg FD would reduce both the overall quality of information (disseminated in general by companies and communicated specifically to securities analysts) and the accessibility and responsiveness of company management.

Analyst opposition to Reg FD centered largely on two issues. First, analysts argued that management-provided information, including information guidance, is a primary means by which companies communicate information to the capital markets. In particular, opponents argued, many companies are more willing to convey complex and potentially proprietary information to securities analysts rather than to issue public disclosures of such information, because analysts have the skill and knowledge to interpret and screen this information. Curtailing such communications between analysts and management would result in no disclosures or simply boilerplate disclosures and would thus diminish the amount and quality of information available to *all* investors, not analysts alone. Second, by reducing the amount of detailed information available to analysts, Reg FD would impair the quality of analysts' reports by reducing the ability of analysts to forecast earnings and make stock recommendations.

In addition to the survey evidence of analysts' beliefs about the expected consequences of Reg FD, a growing body of empirical archival research is now available that has examined the changes in various aspects of companies' information environments between the pre–Reg FD world and the post–Reg FD world. Features of companies' information environments that have been studied include the informativeness of the market for companies' stock and the quality of analyst reports.

Informativeness of the Market for Companies' Stock. Research on the informativeness of the market for companies' stock focuses on documenting changes in three aspects of the capital markets between the pre– and post–Reg FD periods: (1) stock return volatility and trading volume (both on average and in response to specific information), (2) informational efficiency and leaks prior to news events, as reflected in the movements in stock prices prior to the news event, and (3) measures of information asymmetry.

■ *Return volatility.* Research has examined two kinds of volatility in stock market returns—"event return volatility" and "general return volatility." Event volatility captures volatility in response to news events; general volatility captures volatility in event *and* nonevent periods.

When return volatility is examined in response to news events, such as earnings announcements, the researcher is largely capturing a market-based measure of the surprise, or information content, of the news event. When a news event conveys significant information (that is, contains a large surprise component), a larger price reaction is expected than when little information is conveyed. Hence, high volatility in response to an event is considered to indicate a more newsworthy event than low return volatility in response to an event.

Researchers who examine general return volatility are not interested in capturing the information content of news (because for a typical company, news events do not occur on most trading days during the year). They want to measure how information flows to the market. When information flow is smooth and stable, the expectation is for lower general return volatility than when information flow is discrete and infrequent.

Several studies have examined changes in event return volatility of disclosures between the pre– and post–Reg FD periods. Presumably, the interest here is in documenting whether Reg FD has resulted in more or fewer newsworthy disclosures. Within this body of work, the focus has largely been on market reactions to quarterly earnings announcements, although some studies have examined reactions to management earnings forecasts, 8-K filings, conference calls, and analyst reports.

To assess event return volatility, researchers abstract from the direction of the news by taking the absolute value (or squared value) of the market reaction to the news event. The resulting unsigned measure of the market reaction to the event is, essentially, a measure of return volatility. The most common measure of event return volatility is the absolute value of the cumulative abnormal return, *ACAR*, over a short window surrounding the news event, such as a three-day window surrounding the announcement of a company's quarterly earnings (the day before, the day of, and the day after the announcement). The *ACAR* for this window is typically calculated as

$$ACAR(-1,+1)_{j,\,q} = \left| \sum_{t=-1}^{+1} [R_{j,\,t} - E(R_{j,\,t})] \right|, \tag{3.1}$$

where

$ACAR(-1, +1)_{j,q}$ = the absolute value of the cumulative abnormal return to company j's earnings announcement for quarter q, with day $t = 0$ as the day company j announced event q

$R_{j,t}$ = company j's raw return on day t

$E(R_{j,t})$ = company j's expected return on day t

Expected returns are proxied by the market return, a beta-adjusted market return, a size-adjusted market return, or a three-factor adjusted return. The choice of measure to use largely depends on how important the researcher believes it is to control for risk factors affecting company *j*'s returns.[34]

At least five studies have examined event return volatility around quarterly earnings announcements made before versus after the implementation of Reg FD: Bailey, Li, Mao, and Zhong (2003); Eleswarapu, Thompson, and Venkataraman (2004); Gadarowski and Sinha (2002); Heflin, Subramanyam, and Zhang (2003a); Shane, Soderstrom, and Yoon (2001). In all these studies, the authors found significantly *lower* event return volatility around earnings announcements in post–Reg FD periods than in pre–Reg FD periods. Importantly, however, Bailey et al. found that the lower event return volatility does not appear to be an effect of Reg FD; rather, it was caused by decimalization of the stock exchanges, which occurred at roughly the same time as the implementation of Reg FD.[35] Controlling for decimalization, Bailey et al. found no incremental effect of Reg FD on event return volatility around earnings announcements.

Heflin et al. (2003b) examined whether general return volatility changed following implementation of Reg FD. Their measure of general return volatility was similar to that described in Equation 3.1 except Heflin et al. used the squared value (rather than the absolute value) of the company's abnormal returns and their window was not restricted to a short interval around earnings announcement dates. They compared both the total daily return volatility and the average per day return volatility of their sample companies for all trading days in the three quarters preceding Reg FD and the three quarters following Reg FD. Their results showed no evidence that Reg FD has increased general return volatility; in fact, they found the opposite. Both total and per day return volatility declined significantly in the post–Reg FD period relative to the pre–Reg FD period. This result suggests that critics' predictions that Reg FD would increase return volatility were not realized.

---

[34]Subtracting the market return implies that the researcher believes company *j* is as risky as the market (i.e., has a beta of 1). Subtracting the beta-adjusted market return means that the researcher believes the appropriate model of expected return is the capital asset pricing model, which expresses the company's return as a function of that company's covariation with the market return, as captured by its estimated beta. Beta is usually estimated over some relatively short period (e.g., two years) prior to the event. Subtracting the size-adjusted return means that the researcher believes the best measure of the company's expected return is the return earned on similar-size companies, where size is measured by the companies' market capitalization. Finally, subtracting the expected return from the Fama and French (1993) three-factor model means that the researcher believes the company's expected return is best captured by the sum of the company's covariation with the return to (1) the market portfolio, (2) a size portfolio, and (3) a portfolio based on book-to-market ratios. Usually, for short windows (e.g., one, two, or three days), the choice of the measure of expected return has little effect on the results.

[35]Decimalization of stock trading (which occurred in January 2001 for most stocks) reduced tick sizes to 1 cent on all U.S. stock exchanges (the New York and American exchanges and NASDAQ).

▨ *Informational efficiency.* Closely related to the concept of newsworthiness, as captured by event return volatility, is the concept of informational efficiency. Informational efficiency refers to the speed and extent to which stock prices anticipate information in upcoming information events. When stock prices reflect information early and fully, the market is said to be highly *informationally efficient* with respect to the information reported in the upcoming disclosure. In contrast, when the stock market reflects little anticipation of the news (stock prices do not adjust to the information until the release of the disclosure), the market is said to be highly *informationally inefficient* with respect to that disclosure.

Measures of informational efficiency provide a way to calibrate the aggregate effects of private and public disclosures on security prices and, hence, provide a mechanism for evaluating the net effect of Reg FD on *total* information flows. Understanding this net effect is important in light of critics' claims that Reg FD would, on balance, reduce information flows between companies and the market. If these claims were justified, one would expect a decrease in informational efficiency after implementation of Reg FD.

Informational efficiency is measured as the gap between a "full-information" stock price (usually measured one or two days after the news event to ensure that the market has fully impounded the information) and the pre-event price, measured over various windows prior to the announced event. For example, in their analysis of informational efficiency prior to quarterly earnings announcements, Heflin et al. (2003a) examined pre-event periods extending as much as 65 days prior to the earnings announcement date. The specific metric the authors examined is related to the measure of event return volatility, except that it captures the absolute cumulative abnormal return activity over longer windows prior to and including the announcement. Their measure of absolute cumulative abnormal return activity was

$$ACAR(-m,+2)_{j,\,q} = \left| \prod_{t\,=\,-m}^{+2} [1 + R_{j,\,t} - E(R_{j,\,t})] - 1 \right|, \tag{3.2}$$

where $-m$ denotes the number of days prior to the news event.

Before considering the findings of Heflin et al. (2003a), consider how this measure of informational efficiency behaves under extreme assumptions about information flows to the market. Note, first, that greater (lesser) informational efficiency means a smaller (larger) gap between the full-information stock price and the pre-event stock price; this smaller (larger) gap translates into smaller (larger) measures of *ACAR*. For example, consider the two situations presented in **Figure 3.1**. In Situation A, the market is completely uninformed about the upcoming announcement (of bad news) and remains uninformed until the announcement occurs. In this setting, *ACAR* will be large over the entire pre-event window (defined here as Day –65 to Day –1) and will converge to zero

Figure 3.1.   Measuring Informational Efficiency with ACAR

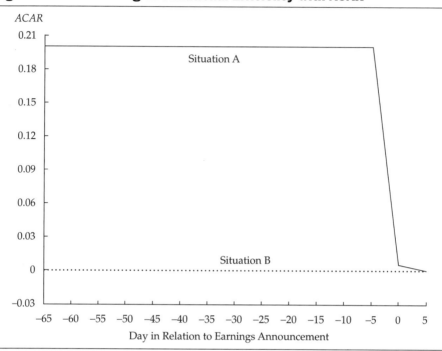

only when the announcement occurs (Day 0) and the news is impounded in the stock price. Now, consider Situation B in Figure 3.1, in which the market fully anticipates at Day –65 the information to be disclosed on Day 0. Because at Day –65 the stock price correctly impounds this information, no further adjustments to stock price occur during the pre-event window or in response to the announcement event itself. In this setting, *ACAR* will be near or equal to zero over the entire interval. Situation A corresponds to the most extreme case of informational inefficiency; Situation B corresponds to the most extreme case of informational efficiency. Of course, most companies' stock returns do not exhibit either of these extreme behaviors but something in between.

Heflin et al. (2003a) calculated and contrasted the *ACAR* measure of informational efficiency for quarterly earnings announcements preceding and following implementation of Reg FD. An illustration of their main findings is given in **Figure 3.2**. As the graph lines clearly show, they found *smaller* average *ACAR*s for earnings announcements made after Reg FD went into effect. That is, the post–Reg FD *ACAR*s lie consistently below the pre–Reg FD *ACAR*s. Results based on median values showed a similar pattern. Overall, this pattern of results is not consistent with critics' claims that Reg FD would reduce total information flows to the market; rather, it is consistent with the view that Reg FD improved informational efficiency.

Figure 3.2.   Informational Efficiency of Earnings Announcements Pre– and Post–Reg FD

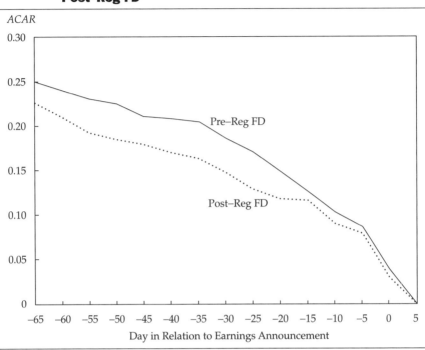

Note: Measurements made for three quarters before and three quarters after implementation of Reg FD.
Source: Heflin, Subramanyam, and Zhang (2003a, Figure 1).

Informational efficiency is linked to the notion of information leakage—information becoming known, intentionally or unintentionally, to a select group of market participants prior to the public disclosure of the information. The more leakage that occurs, the more stock prices are expected to adjust to the upcoming news prior to the news event. Of course, the extent to which leaked information is impounded in stock prices will depend on both the extent to which the leaked information is public knowledge (that is, the size of the set of market participants with knowledge of the leaked information) and the intensity with which these participants trade on this information (or disseminate the information to investors who trade).

Leakage appears to have been of direct interest to regulators in writing Reg FD, because one of their concerns was "leveling the playing field" for favored market participants and individual (retail) investors. The spirit of this claim is that favored market participants, such as securities analysts or institutional investors, may use the private communications from management to trade (or provide the information to others who may trade) in advance of the information being made known to all investors. Presumably, such trading results in favored market participants profiting from their superior access to private communications. Investors without access to the private communications are forced to wait until the information is disclosed publicly by the company or until it becomes public knowledge indirectly when sufficient trading by favored investors causes the stock price to fully reflect the information. In either case, less-favored investors probably profit less, or not at all, than the favored investors. If Reg FD was successful in leveling the playing field, research should find less evidence of information leakage after implementation of Reg FD.

Although leakage is related to informational efficiency—that is, more leakage should, all else being equal, lead to the appearance of greater informational efficiency—researchers cannot discern leakage by using measures of informational efficiency (such as *ACAR*) because these measures do not distinguish between private and public flows of information to the market. In particular, if all flows of information to the market reflected private communications, Heflin et al.'s (2003a) finding of smaller post–Reg FD *ACAR*s would be consistent with greater leakage of information following Reg FD. But because *ACAR*s are affected by *both* public and private information, an equally compelling explanation for the smaller post–Reg FD *ACAR*s is that the amount of public disclosure of upcoming information increased. Indeed, Heflin et al. (2003a) asserted exactly that interpretation when they argued that their results show that Reg FD *increased* information flows.

To focus on information leakage, a researcher would ideally isolate movements in stock prices attributable to private information flows from movements in prices attributable to public information. Unfortunately, it is not possible to design a clean test of this ideal type because private information flows cannot be identified; precisely because they are private, they are not observable. So, to disentangle the effects of public from private information on stock price movements, researchers use two indirect approaches. First, they may focus on relatively short windows just prior to the news event (for example, 2, 5, or 10 days prior to the earnings announcement) and assume that any stock price movements in that window are a result of information leakage. This approach is typically implemented after excluding observations for which public disclosures occurred during the chosen pre-event window, such as preannouncements of the upcoming earnings. The second approach correlates preannouncement stock price movements with announcement-period stock price movements. In this approach, a positive correlation is interpreted as evidence of information leakage.[36]

---

[36]A finding of a positive correlation is consistent with leakage but not determinative of leakage because public disclosures during the preannouncement period could also lead to a positive relationship between preannouncement and announcement-period returns.

Gadarowski and Sinha used both approaches to test whether Reg FD altered the extent of information leakage prior to voluntary earnings forecasts and forecast guidance made by managers. Their preannouncement period was defined as Days (–2, –1), and the announcement period was defined as Days (0, +1); hence, they focused on leakage that occurs near news events. Their results showed that preannouncement abnormal returns are positively correlated with announcement-period abnormal returns and that the amount of preannouncement abnormal return (both in total and as a proportion of the announcement-period abnormal return) has been significantly smaller since Reg FD. Also, for a sample of quarterly earnings announcements, Mac (2002) reported evidence of a decline in information leakage between pre– and post– Reg FD periods. In addition, both studies documented that these effects were more pronounced for large companies than for small companies. They interpreted their results as indicating that Reg FD has been effective in leveling the playing field, especially for investors in large companies, by reducing the extent to which companies can engage in selective disclosures.

▓ *Information asymmetry.* Measures of information asymmetry in the stock market attempt to capture the extent of informed versus uninformed trading in a stock. High information asymmetry reflects a large gap between the knowledge possessed by informed traders and that possessed by uninformed traders. When information asymmetry is high for a stock, uninformed traders prefer not to trade in that stock because of the strong likelihood that informed traders will take advantage of them and because high levels of information asymmetry generally imply higher transaction costs. The absence of trading by uninformed traders reduces the liquidity of the stock.

Common measures of the extent of information asymmetry among investors are the bid–ask spread, a score based on the likelihood of informed trading in the stock, and measures of informed trading based on trade size.

Turning first to bid–ask spreads, we note that spreads have three components—an inventory cost component (reflecting the cost to the market maker of holding the stock in inventory), a transaction cost component (reflecting the cost to trade), and an adverse selection component (reflecting the cost to the market maker of trading with an informed trader). The last of these components—adverse selection—is the component of the spread that can be related to the notion of information asymmetry among investors.

Research on changes in bid–ask spreads in response to Reg FD have generally found mixed results. For example, Eleswarapu et al. and Sunder (2002) documented some evidence of a decline in total spreads following Reg FD, but Eleswarapu et al. found that this effect occurred only for stocks that also experienced decimalization. For a smaller sample of companies, Straser (2002) identified the adverse selection component of the total spread and compared the magnitude of this component pre–Reg FD with the magnitude post–Reg FD. He documented a significant increase in adverse selection following the implementation of Reg FD.

Brown, Hillegeist, and Lo (2002) and Straser found a significant increase in PIN scores following Reg FD. PIN scores, developed by Easley, Kiefer, and O'Hara (1997), capture the "probability of informed" trading in a stock and are based on inferring informed trades from transactional stock data. Although an increase in PIN scores is consistent with an increase in the adverse selection component of the bid–ask spread (found by Straser), Brown, Hillegeist, and Lo noted that the increase in PIN scores is also consistent with a general upward trend in PIN scores that occurred over the same period as the implementation of Reg FD.

An alternative measure of informed trading that researchers have attempted is to characterize the identity of traders based on the size of their trades. Essentially, this research considers low dollar trades (usually trades less than $10,000) as attributable to individual investors and trades in excess of the cutoff amount (or some higher threshold) as attributable to institutional investors. Given that institutional investors generally have greater access to information about a company (partly, at least, because of the security analysts who work for the institution), researchers often characterize institutional traders as being more sophisticated and more informed than individual traders.[37]

Bushee, Matsumoto, and Miller (2002) investigated pre- and post–Reg FD changes in individual trading during conference calls. Using the percentage of a company's total trades that were small (i.e., less than $10,000 in value) as their measure of individual trading, they found that individuals have increased their trading since implementation of Reg FD. The increase in individual trading was more pronounced for companies that had hosted closed conference calls in the pre–Reg FD period, which suggests that Reg FD has had a larger effect on these companies than on companies that had always held open conference calls. The implication of this result is that Reg FD increased individual investors' access to information in conference calls (and the timing of that access) to a level similar to the access and timing of their institutional investor counterparts.

---

[37] A problem with identifying informed and uninformed traders from trade size is that a truly informed trader may mask his or her possession of information by breaking up the trade into smaller pieces and thus appearing to be an uninformed trader. For this reason, tests using measures of uninformed trading derived from trade size are generally of low statistical power.

Quality of Analysts' Reports. If Reg FD was effective in substituting public disclosures for the private communications between managers and securities analysts, Reg FD should have resulted in a shift from private communications to public disclosures. If information flows to analysts were reduced by Reg FD, the quality and newsworthiness of analysts' forecasts should have declined. Have researchers observed a decline in the quality and newsworthiness of analyst reports?

Numerous studies have examined the effects of Reg FD on three properties of analysts' earnings forecasts—accuracy, dispersion, and newsworthiness. Investigations of these characteristics are motivated by the following argument: Critics have argued that because Reg FD eliminated private communications between managers and analysts, analysts' reports should have become less insightful and, therefore, less useful to investors since Reg FD. If individual investors rely on securities analysts as a primary source of company-specific investing information, a decline in the quality of analysts' reports would cause investors to be worse off since the regulation's implementation. This argument rests on the premise that analysts would either be unwilling or unable to replace the information lost by Reg FD's elimination of private communications.

Survey evidence indicates that analysts expected to compensate for the lost private communications with managers. In particular, the majority of analysts responding to the AIMR 2001 survey believed that the accuracy of their earnings forecasts and their stock recommendations would *not* suffer as a result of Reg FD. This evidence suggests that securities analysts believed they would be able to replace the lost management-provided information by searching for other private information.[38] Research into the effects of Reg FD on the quality of analysts' reports explores not only whether the changes in quality materialized but also whether analysts were able to substitute other information for the lost communications with management.

Probably the most unambiguous measure of forecast quality is forecast accuracy, measured as the absolute value of the forecast error. At least five studies to date have looked for any change in the accuracy of analysts' EPS forecasts between the pre– and post–Reg FD periods: Agrawal and Chadha (2003); Bailey et al.; Heflin et al. (2003a); Mohanram and Sunder (2001); Shane et al. Three of the studies (Bailey et al.; Heflin et al.; Shane et al.) found no change in forecast accuracy, whereas the other two (Agrawal and Chandha; Mohanram and Sunder) found a decrease in forecast accuracy. Mohanram

---

[38]Survey evidence reported by Janvrin and Kurtenbach (2002), however, indicated that 51 percent of analysts believed the amount of financial information provided by company managers decreased following Reg FD; 14 percent believed it was unchanged.

and Sunder further found that the decline in forecast accuracy is more pronounced for the less-skilled analysts; in particular, they found that All-Star analysts (as defined by the *Institutional Investor* annual ranking of analysts) experienced a smaller average increase in absolute forecast errors than did non-All-Star analysts.

A second property of analysts' forecasts is their dispersion. Dispersion captures the extent of disagreement among analysts about a particular company's earnings for a given quarter. Recall from Chapter 1 that dispersion is viewed as a proxy for the degree of heterogeneity of beliefs (among analysts following the same company) with respect to earnings expectations. The greater the variation among analysts' earnings forecasts for a given company-quarter, the more uncertainty and, therefore, the less confidence that the consensus of those forecasts is a good measure of the market's expectation for earnings. At least seven studies have examined the effect of Reg FD on analyst forecast dispersion. Two of these studies (Heflin et al. 2003a; Shane et al.) found no change in forecast dispersion between the pre– and post–Reg FD periods, whereas five (Agrawal and Chadha; Bailey et al.; Irani and Karamanou 2003; Mohanram and Sunder; Topaloglu 2002) reported a significant increase in dispersion following implementation of Reg FD.

A third property of analysts' forecasts is their newsworthiness. Recall from Chapter 1 that a common proxy for newsworthiness is the absolute price impact of the analyst's report on the day it is issued. In comparing the price impact of analysts' reports between the pre– and post–Reg FD periods, Gintschel and Markov (2003) documented a significant decline. They reported that the average price impact of analysts' reports was 32 percent lower in the post–Reg FD period than in the pre–Reg FD period.

Although these studies interpreted the smaller newsworthiness and the greater dispersion of analysts forecasts as suggesting that Reg FD had the intended effect of reducing selective disclosure (that is, of reducing the flow of private information), their results do not prove such effects. In particular, several studies noted that these findings could be the result of changes in *either* the amount of private information or the amount of public information. This distinction is important because it concerns two very different explanations for the increased dispersion in analysts' forecasts. One explanation is that the increased dispersion is the result of larger amounts of public information in the post–Reg FD period. Larger amounts of public information may have occurred for several reasons, not the least of which relate to the crash of the Internet bubble in October 2000 and to the start of the economic recession in March 2001. The other explanation is that the increased dispersion is the result of *increased* private information in the post–Reg FD period as analysts make efforts to replace the private communications from client managers with other sources. Importantly, only the latter explanation (analysts expanding efforts to acquire private information) is causally linked to Reg FD; the former explanation (larger amounts of public information because of economic shocks) is not.

Two studies using different approaches have attempted to parse these two effects. Mohanram and Sunder used a methodology developed by Barron, Kim, Lim, and Stevens (1998) to separate the private and public information components of analysts' forecasts. Their approach combined information contained in analysts' forecast errors and forecast dispersion to create measures of the extent to which analysts rely on public information versus private information in developing their forecasts. Applying these measures to their sample, Mohanram and Sunder found that the amount of public information in analysts' forecasts declined after Reg FD but the amount of private information increased. They concluded that since Reg FD, analysts are expending more time and effort to enhance the quality of their private information about a given company.

Zitzewitz (2002) noted that the approach used by Mohanram and Sunder is limited because it does not distinguish between "herding" behavior and rapid changes in consensus expectations (which probably occurred during the Internet crash and the 2001 recession).[39] Using a methodology that does not suffer from these limitations, Zitzewitz found results that are the opposite of Mohanram and Sunder's findings. Specifically, he found that a dramatic decrease occurred post–Reg FD in the amount of private information and a substantial increase occurred in the amount of public information. His results, therefore, are more consistent with the view that greater disclosure of public information (not enhanced private information search or processing) led to the increased dispersion in post–Reg FD forecasts.

Inferring Causality from Pre– vs. Post–Reg FD Studies. All of the Reg FD studies described to this point used a similar research design. The approach was to compare proxies for the information environment measured in one or more pre–Reg FD periods with similar proxies measured in one or more post–Reg FD periods. Typically, the pre– and post–Reg FD periods were chosen to avoid the quarter in which Reg FD took effect (the fourth calendar quarter of 2000). Most studies defined the pre–Reg FD period to include the three, four, or five quarters ending prior to the quarter in which Reg FD was implemented and defined the post–Reg FD period as the same quarters for periods following implementation. [Matching the quarter q (= 1, 2, 3, and 4) earnings forecasted in year t with the quarter q earnings forecast for year $t + 1$ controls for any seasonality in the information proxies.]

---

[39] We discuss herding behavior in Chapter 4.

In general, this type of company-specific, pre versus post research design works well if no confounding factors occurred at the same time as the event under study. In the case of Reg FD, such an assumption is highly questionable. In the time period covered by Reg FD research (1998–2001), several events occurred that could, and probably did, affect inferences about companies' information environments:

- the beginning of the economic recession in the United States (March 2001),
- the crash of the Internet bubble (beginning October 2000),
- the decimalization of stock trading on U.S. stock exchanges (late January 2001 for most stocks),
- the demise of Enron Corporation (beginning in September 2001 and ending on 1 December 2001 when the company filed for Chapter 11 protection) and Arthur Andersen (indicted in March 2002, found guilty in June 2002, and ceased audits of SEC registrants as of 31 August 2002), and
- general trends in technology, movements through business cycles, and changes in macroeconomic indicators, such as interest rates and gross domestic product (GDP).

The potential confluence of these events makes drawing a causal connection between any change in the information environment and Reg FD extremely difficult. In particular, the existence of these other economywide changes means that any of these explanations is as likely as Reg FD to have caused an observed change in the information environment.

The key to resolving this inference problem is to control for the effects of the other economywide changes. Some studies have attempted to do so by including, as independent variables, measures of industry performance (such as growth or profitability), interest rates, or GDP. This approach is limited to those explanations that can be proxied by some readily measurable variable (such as GDP). Other studies have focused on one alternative explanation and attempt to exploit variation in that explanation to identify the effects of Reg FD. A good example of this approach is Bailey et al.'s analysis of the effects of decimalization on measures of return volatility. Although this approach sheds light on the one alternative explanation studied, it does not address the possibility that other explanations may lie behind the results.

A third approach seeks to identify cross-sectional variation in the degree to which companies were likely to be affected by Reg FD. An example is Bushee et al.'s analysis of the *relative effects* of Reg FD on companies that had previously held open versus closed conference calls. The advantage of this approach is that it allows the researcher to identify *ex ante* companies for which the larger effects would be expected. For example, Bushee et al. argued that Reg FD should have had bigger effects on companies that formerly held closed conference calls because it forced these companies either to stop holding closed conference calls or to open them. The limitation of this approach is that it hinges on the *difference* in the degree to which two groups of companies (i.e., previously "closed" versus previously "open") are expected to respond to Reg FD.

Francis, Nanda, and Wang (2004) adopted this third approach but identified companies for which the authors expected extreme variation in responses to Reg FD. Their design exploited the fact that not all companies traded on the U.S. stock exchanges were subject to Reg FD. In particular, they noted that Rule 101(b) of Reg FD explicitly excludes foreign issuers trading on U.S. exchanges. Practically, the effect is that Canadian companies and companies that trade as American Depositary Receipts (ADRs) are excluded from Reg FD (hereafter, we will refer to all such companies as "ADRs" for simplicity).[40] Francis, Nanda, and Wang identified ADRs in the same industry and of similar size as U.S.-listed companies and compared the resulting one-to-one matched samples in terms of the effects of Reg FD. If changes over time in ADRs' information environments capture all changes that are *not* a result of Reg FD, this approach allows the authors to interpret any difference between the information environments of the matched U.S. companies relative to the ADR companies as capturing the effects of Reg FD. The power of this approach depends on whether ADRs responded to Reg FD even though they were not required to do so. Anecdotal and empirical results suggest that although ADR companies responded some, they responded significantly less than U.S. companies that were not exempt from this regulation.

Francis, Nanda, and Wang found no evidence that Reg FD has had any material effect on return volatility (event or general), trading volume, informational efficiency, forecast dispersion, or forecast newsworthiness. Specifically, they found that changes after Reg FD in these information properties experienced by companies that are subject to Reg FD are indistinguishable from the changes experienced by companies that are not required to comply with this regulation. Unless exempt companies felt as compelled to respond to Reg FD as their nonexempt counterparts, these findings suggest that Reg FD has had no effect on the information environments of affected companies.

---

[40]Canadian companies that choose to be listed on the U.S. exchanges do not trade as ADRs but are directly listed. Although Canadian law prohibits selective disclosures, these laws have, apparently, not been enforced. Indeed, as late as July 2002, the Ontario Securities Commission released guidance for selective disclosures saying, "Canadian law has specifically prohibited selective disclosure for decades, but Canadian companies needed guidance on what terms such as 'necessary course of business' actually meant." ("Canadian Regulator . . ." 2002)

Summary and Conclusion

Do analysts rely on company managers for information? Did this reliance decrease following implementation of Reg FD? The answer to both questions is surely yes. But the answer to whether this reliance creates a *dependence* by analysts on company-provided information is less obvious because of the lack of direct methods of testing for the effects and benefits of private communications with management. Indirect tests generally show patterns in forecast errors that are consistent with such dependence. That is, empirical evidence to date suggests that analysts issue more optimistic forecasts when facing greater incentives to curry favor with management. At least some portion of this behavior appears warranted; anecdotal evidence and research indicate that analysts who deviate from favorable forecasting experience reprisals in the form of blocked or withheld communications.

The question of whether Reg FD achieved its intended effects remains open. Much of the current research into the effects of this regulation has used a design that does not control well (or at all) for other changes that occurred at the same time as Reg FD. Research that controlled for contemporaneous events (such as decimalization of the stock exchanges, the Internet crash, and the recession) generally reveals no significant differences between pre– and post–Reg FD measures of stock market effects, such as return volatility and informational efficiency.

4. Analyst Independence from Other Analysts

A common belief, based on behavioral studies, is that individuals "herd" in many aspects of their daily lives. Loosely speaking, "herding" refers to behavior patterns that are correlated across individuals (i.e., behavioral clustering). Although behavioral clustering is often taken to imply a lack of independence among individuals, it may also occur when independently acting individuals receive correlated information from independent sources. This type of clustering is usually not considered herding. Rather, the notion of herding considered here, and in most academic research, is similar to that of imitation or mimicry. An individual is herding if the person's decision is influenced by the decision(s) of others. As a social phenomenon, imitation has been documented by numerous studies in zoology, sociology, and social psychology and is perhaps among human beings' most basic instincts.

Academic research and the popular press suggest that market participants herd in their investment decisions. For example, anecdotal evidence has pointed out the overpricing of U.S. technology stocks in the late 1990s and the fact that new equity issues and takeovers occur in waves—both of which are consistent with investor herding. From a financial perspective, the problem with investor herding is that it may lead to an inefficient market if individuals' actions that are not socially optimal influence the behavior of followers—creating a cascade effect.

In addition to investors, financial analysts have also been portrayed as susceptible to herding. Security analysts perform an important intermediation function between publicly traded companies and investors because they analyze and disseminate information about historical and prospective corporate performance to market participants. Therefore, whether security analysts herd has significant implications for the efficiency of information acquisition, processing, and transmission in the financial markets.

The literature on herding behavior in financial markets has grown significantly during the past decade. This chapter provides an introductory discussion to security analysts' herding; we do not mean to provide a comprehensive review of the general literature on herding.[41] We first discuss the existing

---

[41] Readers who are interested in more general herding theories and evidence on herding can consult several excellent survey articles (e.g., Bikhchandani, Hirshleifer, and Welch 1998; Daniel, Hirshleifer, and Teoh 2002; Devenow and Welch 1996; Hirshleifer and Teoh 2003).

theories of individual herding and their relevance to security analysts. Then, we survey empirical evidence that is consistent with analysts' herding. Finally, we discuss the difficulties in discriminating among competing theories for analysts herding and introduce several methods that attempt to overcome these difficulties.

Theory

Two polar views suggest why individuals herd—the irrational view and the rational view. The irrational view states that investors converge in their beliefs or actions "because of a 'herd instinct' or, from a contagious emotional response to stressful events" (Hirshleifer and Teoh 2003, p.1). The rational view proposes that herding is the rational response of individuals to incentives or their information environment. We do not consider irrational perspectives in this chapter, so we turn now to the rational view.

Rational Theories on Herding. Within the rational perspective, researchers have studied various mechanisms that might explain the occurrence of herding. We review four such mechanisms—sanctions on deviants, payoff externalities, career concerns, and information cascades.

◼ *Sanctions on deviants.* The theory of sanctions on deviants holds that individuals herd if they believe they will be punished for deviations from the social norm. Sanctions may lead to persistence of socially inefficient customs; for example, Akerlof (1980) considered a labor market in which the social norm prohibits employers from hiring workers at a reduced wage. Although there may be workers willing to work at the reduced wage, the employer cannot profitably hire these workers because his current workers will not train the new workers; doing so would undermine the current workers' reputation. Akerlof showed that unemployment will persist if individuals are punished by loss of reputation for disobeying the custom.

◼ *Payoff externalities.* Payoff externalities occur when an individual's payoff for adopting a particular action increases as the number of other individuals adopting the same action increases. For example, the benefit from signing up for a specific instant messaging network (for example, AOL, MSN, or Yahoo!) increases as the number of other people who sign up for the same service increases. As a result, individuals have incentives to coordinate their behavior. Diamond and Dybvig (1983) provided an example of how payoff externalities can lead to bank runs. If all depositors rush to withdraw their funds from the bank because of fears that the bank may go bankrupt, the sudden withdrawals will push the bank into bankruptcy even if it is financially sound. Thus, depositors' herding to withdraw their funds is rational because their fear of bankruptcy is self-fulfilling.

■ *Career concerns.* Individuals care how their current performance affects the labor market's beliefs about their abilities and, as a result, their future compensation. Career concerns often provide an individual with implicit incentives for performance. For example, although white-collar employees are typically paid fixed annual salaries, they may be induced to strive for higher performance—despite the absence of explicit incentives—if their current performance affects their future in the company. Specifically, if bad performance increases employees' chances of being fired or if good performance increases their chances of promotion, employees will have implicit incentives to increase their effort and performance. Fama (1980) argued that in a competitive labor market, career concerns will motivate corporate managers even if they are not given explicit pay-for-performance compensation contracts. Holmstrom (1999) modeled these implicit incentives formally and concluded that implicit incentives can substitute (although not perfectly) for such explicit incentives as performance-contingent compensation (e.g., an earnings-based bonus plan).

The effects of career concerns have been analyzed in many settings, including corporate investment decisions (Avery and Chevalier 1999; Milbourn, Shockley, and Thakor 2001; Prendergast and Stole 1996; Scharfstein and Stein 1990), trading patterns of mutual fund managers (Chevalier and Ellison 1999), analysts' forecasting behavior (Chen and Jiang 2004; Ehrbeck and Waldmann 1996; Trueman 1994), and incentives in government agencies (Dewatripont, Jewitt, and Tirole 1999). In general, the effects of career concerns on individual behavior depend on the performance measures being used to evaluate individuals and on how these measures affect future compensation. For example, the study by Scharfstein and Stein and the study by Trueman both show that herding behavior arises as an individual's best response to career concerns. But consider the contrasts in the behavior and the settings of the two studies.

In Scharfstein and Stein, managers faced identical investment choices— a high-NPV (net present value) project or a low-NPV project. The managers could be of high ability or low ability, although neither the managers nor the market observed the true ability of the managers. High-ability managers received correlated information signals on which to base investment decisions. Low-ability managers received uncorrelated, noisy signals that had no investment value. Scharfstein and Stein showed that when any two managers face this investment decision, an equilibrium exists in which the first manager makes his choice based on his signal and the second manager always imitates this choice regardless of her own signal. As a result, the market infers managers' abilities on the basis of whether the managers' investment choices are identical. If the investment choices are the same, the market views the managers as being of high ability; if the investment choices differ, the market infers the managers are of low ability.

The intuition for this result is as follows. If the second manager responds to her own signal, the market correctly infers that her signal differed from the first manager's and infers that both managers are of low ability (because only managers of low ability received uncorrelated signals). If the second manager mimics the first manager's investment choice, however, she increases the likelihood that the market will conclude that both managers have high ability (correlated signals). This outcome is akin to the insight of John Maynard Keynes (1936, p. 158): "Worldly wisdom teaches us that is it better for the reputation to fail conventionally than to succeed unconventionally."

Trueman studied herding in analyst forecasting behavior. In his model, analysts had either high ability or low ability and they knew their own type. The high-ability analysts received more precise signals about a company's future earnings than did the low-ability analysts. Trueman showed that, on average, all analysts tend to issue forecasts that are biased toward the market's prior earnings expectations (i.e., they herd). Low-ability analysts, however, are even more likely to herd—that is, to ignore their own information and to issue forecasts biased toward the prevailing earnings forecast. The intuition for this result is that it is less costly for a low-ability analyst than for a high-ability analyst to ignore information because the low-ability analyst's signals are less informative than the more precise signals received by a high-ability analyst.

A key assumption in both of these studies is that the market is imperfectly informed about the agent's ability. In the Scharfstein and Stein model, the market did not observe the managers' private signals; in the Trueman model, the market did not observe the analysts' true abilities. In both models, the market inferred an agent's ability by comparing her action with that of her peers. Both studies showed that when such imperfect inferences are drawn from other agents' actions, individuals may prefer to mimic the actions of others to preserve or enhance their reputation.

■ *Information cascades.* Loosely speaking, an information cascade occurs when the action of an agent (individual) stops conveying the agent's supporting information to others who act after the agent. Information cascades can occur only when agents act in sequence and when the agents acting later in the sequence cannot observe the information underlying the behavior of agents acting earlier. An information cascade can also be thought of as an information externality. That is, each agent's action conveys information to others who act later, but agents do not consider this effect in choosing their actions. When the behavior of earlier-acting agents does not completely reveal their private information, later-acting agents draw inefficient inferences. When these inferences are imperfect, later-acting agents often ignore their own information and follow the actions of the earlier-acting agents.

Banerjee (1992) provided a classic example of an information cascade. Suppose two restaurants, A and B, are adjacently located. Assume also that the commonly held belief is that, with a probability of 51 percent, Restaurant A is better than Restaurant B (with the probability of 49 percent that B is better than A). Apart from this common prior belief, everyone receives a private signal, of equal precision, indicating which restaurant is better (this private signal could be wrong). Suppose that 99 of 100 people receive the signal that Restaurant B is better but the one person whose signal favors Restaurant A gets to choose first. Clearly, this first person will choose to eat at Restaurant A. The second person (whose private signal favors B) will observe the first person's action and infer that the first person received a signal that favored A. Given that all signals are of equal precision, the second person now confronts contradictory signals that cancel each other. In this case, he will revert to his prior belief (which is based on his observation of the action chosen by the earlier-acting individual) and choose Restaurant A. As a result, the second person's decision does not convey information to the people acting after him about his private signal. The result is that everyone ends up eating at Restaurant A, even though the private information overwhelmingly indicates that Restaurant B is the better choice.

For an information cascade to occur, the agents' possible actions must be discrete. In the restaurant example, the decision is to dine in either Restaurant A or Restaurant B; there is no continuum of restaurant choices. Such discreteness prevents later-acting agents from completely unraveling the information underlying earlier-acting individuals' behavior. To see this effect, consider a situation in which the first person receives either a signal that strongly favors A or a signal that only marginally tilts his preference toward A. If the first person acts differently depending on which of the two signals he observes (which he cannot do if the decision is an either/or decision), then the second person, by observing the first person's action, will make the correct inference from the first person's private signal. But if the first person chooses to go to Restaurant A in case of a strong signal *and* in case of a marginal signal, the private information in her signal is lost.

Analysts' earnings forecasts and price targets, although usually made in cents per share, are substantially less discrete, more of a continuum, than their stock recommendations, which are usually made in a small number of categories from strong sell to strong buy. Thus, if an information cascade occurs among analysts, it is more likely to be observed in their stock recommendations than price targets.

Analysts' Incentives to Herd. Analysts may herd not only in their stock recommendations, earnings forecasts, and price targets but also in other aspects of their reporting behavior, such as the decision on covering a company or the timing of issuing a forecast. Depending on the incentive and information environment analysts face, some of the mechanisms we have mentioned may be more plausible than others in explaining analyst herding.

Trueman showed that career concerns may lead analysts to ignore their private information and herd to the market consensus in their forecasts. An important assumption in his model is that analysts care about their forecast accuracy. Anecdotal evidence and empirical evidence support this assumption. For example, earnings forecast accuracy is one of the four criteria explicitly used by *Institutional Investor* in designating All-America Research Team analysts.[42] Moreover, although earnings forecast accuracy is rarely an explicit factor in analysts' annual compensation, it is implicit in their reward systems. As one analyst put it, "If your estimates aren't accurate, nobody's going to buy your stocks" (Dorfman 1991).

Academic research has provided substantial support for the notion that earnings forecast accuracy affects analysts' career opportunities. Stickel (1992) found that All-America analysts selected by *Institutional Investor* issue more-accurate earnings forecasts and revise their forecasts more frequently than other analysts. This finding suggests that accuracy is rewarded, because All-America analysts are typically better compensated than other analysts.

Several studies have examined how analysts' past forecast accuracy is related to their future career moves. Three measures of career move have been studied: the probability that an analyst will leave the profession, the probability that an analyst will change his or her employer, and the probability that an analyst will move up or move down in his or her next job. Hong, Kubik, and Solomon (2000) found that younger analysts are more likely than their older counterparts to leave the profession because of poor forecast accuracy. Mikhail, Walther, and Willis (1999) found that the probability that an analyst will change employer is higher if the analyst has low forecast accuracy (relative to the analyst's peers) in the prior year. The authors did not find a statistically significant relationship, however, between the probability of an analyst's turnover and the profitability of the analyst's stock recommendations.

On the whole, these findings suggest that forecast accuracy matters to analysts' future careers. They are not conclusive, however, because other reasons may explain an analyst's decision to leave the profession or to change

---

[42]The other criteria are stock picking, written reports, and overall service. The All-America Research Team members are selected by polling several hundred institutional investors and money managers. The results are published annually in *Institutional Investor*'s October issue.

employers. Notably, the analyst may be pursuing a better career opportunity. To address this concern, Hong and Kubik (2003) separated brokerage houses into high-status and low-status houses; they defined "leader houses" as those that employ the most *Institutional Investor* All-America analysts (firms such as Goldman Sachs and Merrill Lynch & Co.). They examined whether better forecast accuracy increases an analyst's chances of moving from a low-status house to a high-status house or of staying at a high-status house. Hong and Kubik found that analysts with high forecast accuracy are more likely to experience a favorable job separation (moving up to or remaining at a high-status brokerage house) than analysts with low forecast accuracy.

Although caring about forecast accuracy may lead analysts to herd, other incentives may lead analysts to "antiherd"—that is, to issue bold forecasts. For example, analysts face pressure to generate brokerage business, with their reward sometimes explicitly tied to the amount of trading commissions they generate. Chen and Jiang (2004) showed that such a reward structure motivates analysts to exaggerate their forecasts (i.e., antiherd). The intuition for this result is straightforward: Investors trade on news and, therefore, are unlikely to trade on a forecast that simply repeats information contained in prior forecasts.

Payoff externalities may induce analysts to herd in the types of companies they cover. In particular, it may be economical for an analyst to initiate coverage of a company when other analysts follow the company if payoff externalities exist such that companies with a large analyst following exhibit lower costs of initiating coverage.

Empirical Evidence

In surveying the empirical evidence on analyst herding behavior, we begin with a discussion of herding by institutional investors, including money managers at pension funds and mutual funds. The investment decisions of these institutions are usually based on the analyses and recommendations of the analysts employed by the institution. Hence, we interpret research on herding by institutional investors to reflect, at least in part, the herding behavior of buy-side analysts. We then discuss evidence of herding in sell-side analysts' work products, including their stock recommendations, earnings forecasts, and the timing of their forecasts. In our discussions, we highlight the difficulties of documenting herding. Specifically, how can one know with confidence that herding exists? Because confidence in these inferences depends on the adequacy of the test variables and the research design, we also provide brief discussions of the methodologies used to measure herding.

Herding by Institutional Investors. Much anecdotal evidence suggests that investors herd in their investment decisions; in particular, they follow the investment decisions made by influential investors. For example, investors tend to mimic the investment choices of such influential investors as Long-Term Capital Management (before its collapse) or Warren Buffett (see Lohse 1998). According to the *Economist* (see Silverfinger 1998), silver prices soared with the disclosure that Buffett had bought approximately 20 percent of the 1997 world silver output. As another example, O'Brien and Murray (1995) noted that share prices for American Express Company and PNC Bank increased by, respectively, 4.3 percent and 3.6 percent when Buffett's filings indicated he had increased his shareholding in these companies.

Despite anecdotal evidence, large-sample empirical evidence of herding is inconclusive. The main difficulty in documenting herding is the need to rule out clustering in actions because of common information. That is, it is hard to eliminate the possibility that some external factor is independently influencing investors' trading decisions. For example, it would be inappropriate to conclude that analysts are herding if all analysts revise their earnings forecasts upward for a pharmaceutical company upon learning that the company's new drug received U.S. Federal Drug Administration approval; for all analysts to revise their forecasts in that circumstance is rational.

Early studies investigated whether the trading decisions of institutions were correlated and reached different conclusions. For example, Kraus and Stoll (1972), using data from a U.S. Securities and Exchange Commission study on monthly changes in institutional stock holdings, found little evidence of herding. In a related study, Friend, Blume, and Crockett (1970) found that mutual funds tend to buy stocks that were purchased by successful funds in the previous quarter, which is consistent with herding.

More-recent studies have used a statistical measure of herding developed by Lakonishok, Shleifer, and Vishny (1992; hereafter, LSV). LSV measured herding as the average tendency of a group of individuals to buy/sell particular stocks at the same time relative to what would be expected if these individuals traded independently. Usually, this group of investors has similar characteristics; for example, they might be pension fund managers.

The method was as follows: Let $B_{i,t}(S_{i,t})$ be the number of fund managers in a given group who buy (sell) stock i in quarter t. The LSV measure of herding for stock i in quarter t by this group of investors is

$$LSV_{i,t} = |p_{i,t} - p_t| - AdjFactor_i, \tag{4.1}$$

where $p_{i,t}$ is the proportion of all investors in the group trading stock i in quarter t that are buyers and is calculated as $B_{i,t}/(B_{i,t} + S_{i,t})$. The variable p_t is the average of $p_{i,t}$ over all $i = 1,...,I$ stocks traded by at least one of the fund managers in the group in the same quarter. Intuitively, the first term in the LSV measure, $|p_{i,t} - p_t|$, captures the "unexpected buys" for stock i in quarter t (with the "expected buys" given by the average buys by the fund managers for all stocks in the same time period). For example, suppose all fund managers traded only IBM Corporation, Microsoft Corporation, and Dell and that in a given quarter, 80 percent of the fund managers bought IBM, 70 percent bought Microsoft and 60 percent bought Dell. Then, the expected buys, p_t, would be 70 percent (the average of 80 percent, 70 percent, and 60 percent) and the unexpected buys for IBM would be 10 percent (80 percent – 70 percent).

Unexpected buys can occur for various reasons—planned increases in the fund's holdings, the arrival of unexpected favorable information, and/or herding by institutional investors. To control for effects other than herding, LSV modified the calculation of unexpected buys by subtracting an adjustment factor, $AdjFactor_i$, which allows for random variation around the expected proportion of buyers under the null hypothesis of independent fund trading. Empirically, $AdjFactor_i$ is calculated as the average of unexpected buys over all other quarters. In the preceding example, the adjustment factor would be determined by repeating the $|p_{IBM,t} - p_t|$ calculation to obtain the unexpected buys for IBM for all other quarters, averaging those values across all quarters (to obtain $AdjFactor_i$), and then subtracting the adjustment from $|p_{IBM,t} - p_t|$.

LSV applied their measure to investigate herding behavior in the investment decisions made by 341 money managers at 769 U.S. pension funds. The average value of the herding measure for their sample was 2.7, indicating that if 100 funds traded in a given stock-quarter, 2.7 more funds traded on the same side of the market than would be expected under the null hypothesis that the funds picked stocks independently. Although 2.7 is reliably different from 0, it is small in economic terms. LSV found that herding behavior is more pronounced in small-capitalization stocks. They interpreted this result as suggesting that the poorer information environments of small-cap stocks lead money managers to pay relatively more attention to the actions of other players in making their own investment decisions.

Grinblatt, Titman, and Wermers (1995) used the LSV measure to examine the trading behavior of 274 mutual funds between 1974 and 1984. They also found little evidence of (economically significant) herding. When they partitioned their sample on the basis of the past performance of stocks, they found that funds exhibit greater herding in buying past winners than in selling past losers. Grinblatt et al. also defined a herding measure at the fund level. Of the seven types of funds they considered (balanced funds, growth and income funds, growth funds, aggressive-growth funds, income funds, special-purpose funds, and venture capital/special situation funds), they found that aggressive-growth funds exhibit the highest tendency to herd, with growth funds ranked second.

Wermers (1999) conducted a similar analysis on a substantially larger sample—all mutual funds that existed between 1975 and 1994. He found evidence of herding on average, and this herding was more pronounced for small-cap stocks, for stocks that had experienced high returns, and for funds that were growth oriented. Contrary to the findings of Grinblatt et al., Wermers found that, on average in his sample, herds formed more often on the sell side of the market than on the buy side; this behavior was especially pronounced for small-cap stocks. He also found superior performance among the stocks that "herds" bought relative to those they sold during the six months subsequent to trades, especially among small-cap stocks.

Investor herding has also been examined in an international context. In studying investors' trading strategies in the South Korean stock market, Kim and Wei (1999) found evidence of significant herding by nonresident investors and institutional investors. They also found that herds of nonresident institutional investors formed more easily for the 19 Korean stocks that were regularly reported in the *Wall Street Journal* and for stocks that showed extreme returns in the previous month. Choe, Kho, and Stultz (1999) documented similar findings for the Korean market.

Partly because of limitations of the LSV measure, other researchers have proposed and tested alternative measures of herding.[43] One such measure considers whether the returns on individual stocks cluster more tightly around the market return during large price changes. Tight clustering of stocks around the market during periods of market stress is interpreted as evidence that investors prefer to treat all stocks similarly during such periods rather than choose individual stocks. Using this measure of clustering, Christie and Huang (1995) found a relatively higher dispersion of stocks around the market return at times of large price movements. Because reduced dispersion would be consistent with a herding argument, the authors interpreted this result as inconsistent with investor herding.

---

[43]As to the limitations of the LSV measure, Bikhachandani and Sharma (2001) pointed out three. First, the measure uses the *number of investors* and does not consider the *value of stock* that investors buy or sell. Second, it does not capture whether herding is constant over time (that is, do the same sets of funds herd?). Third, it is sensitive to the frequency with which fund managers trade. In particular, if the average time between trades is three months or more, quarterly data may be sufficient to detect herding, but if the average time between trades is a month or less, a quarterly interval, corresponding to most of the data publicly available to researchers, is too long a time period.

Nofsinger and Sias (1999) used the correlation between stock returns and changes in institutional investors' holdings of the stocks to assess the impact of herding. They found a strong positive correlation between the two variables. They interpreted this finding as consistent with the herding of institutional investors having a greater effect on stock prices than the herding of individual investors.

Brown, Harlow, and Starks (1996) and Chevalier and Ellison (1997) found that mutual fund managers that are doing well lock in their gains toward the end of the year by indexing their funds to the market; funds that are doing poorly deviate from the benchmark, possibly in an attempt to beat it. Later, Chevalier and Ellison (1999) examined whether reputation and career concerns induce herding. Using Morningstar data for managers of growth and growth and income funds during the 1992–95 period, they found that junior managers chose portfolios that were more "conventional" and had lower nonsystematic risk than the portfolios of the senior managers. The authors interpreted these results as consistent with herding behavior among junior fund managers.

Herding in Analysts' Stock Recommendations. Graham (1999) examined whether the tendency of investment newsletters to herd around Value Line's investment recommendations is consistent with a herding model based on career concerns. His sample included more than 5,000 recommendations made by 237 newsletters during 1980–1992. Using the *Value Line Investment Survey* to provide the "market leaders," he examined how characteristics of a newsletter writer affect the writer's tendency to change a recommended equity weight in the same direction as that recommended by Value Line. Graham found that the ability of the newsletter writer is the key factor in determining whether his or her recommendation herds on Value Line. Measuring newsletter ability by the proportion of correct forecasts the newsletter writer had made, Graham found that the newsletter writers with less ability are more likely to herd.[44] Graham also showed that herding is more likely if the reputation of the newsletter writer is high, if prior information is strongly held, and if informative signals are highly correlated.

Welch (2000) used more than 44,000 recommendations between 1989 and 1994 from Zacks Investment Research database to examine whether analysts herd in their stock recommendations. Unlike the distribution of the newsletter recommendations studied by Graham, the distribution of sell-side analysts'

---

[44]Graham viewed a forecast as correct (incorrect) if the writer recommended increasing (decreasing) equity weights in period t and the monthly market excess return in period $t + 1$ was positive (negative).

stock recommendations in the Welch study was highly skewed: Many more buy and strong buy recommendations were made than sell or strong sell recommendations. In Welch's sample, more than 48 percent of the recommendations were buy or strong buy, compared with about 9 percent sell or strong sell recommendations. Furthermore, he found more upward revisions than downward revisions, making the probability of a revised recommendation highly asymmetrical. For example, the probability that a current sell recommendation would be revised to a buy was 54 percent, whereas the probability that a current strong buy recommendation would be revised to a buy was only 27 percent. Because of this asymmetrical distribution, a linear regression (which assumes a symmetrical distribution) was unsuitable.

The asymmetrical nature of the distribution of recommendation revisions would not be a problem if a theory had been developed as to what the distribution looks like under the null hypothesis of no herding. If one knows what the no-herding distribution looks like, one can compare the observed empirical distribution with the no-herding benchmark distribution and determine whether any clustering can be attributed to herding. Unfortunately, no theory yet exists that characterizes the no-herding distribution.

For these reasons, Welch developed a statistical procedure to parse out the effects of herding and no-herding behavior. His method exploits time-series variability in the consensus forecast. Specifically, he argued that a high frequency of revisions from sell to buy is not evidence of herding when the consensus is a buy recommendation but a high frequency of revisions from sell to buy is evidence of herding when the consensus is a hold or a strong buy. Although this classification of herding is conservative (it may fail to detect herding when herding exists), it minimizes the chance of inferring herding when herding does not exist.

In Welch's procedure, the parameter Θ is the measure of herding behavior. He assumed that the herding parameter affects the probability that a recommendation of i is revised to a recommendation of j [that is, $\mathrm{Pr}_{i,j}(\Theta,T)$] as follows:

$$\mathrm{Pr}_{i,j}(\theta, T) \equiv \mathrm{Pr}_{i,j}(0) \left\{ \frac{\left[1 + (j - T)^2\right]^{-\theta}}{D_i} \right\}, \tag{4.2}$$

where

$$D_i = \sum_{j=1}^{5} p_{i,j}(0)\left[1 + (j - T)^2\right]^{-\theta} \tag{4.3}$$

and T is the prevailing consensus recommendation. Thus,

$$\Pr_{i,j}(0) \equiv \Pr_{i,j}(0,T) \tag{4.4}$$

is the unconditional probability of a recommendation revision from i to j under the null hypothesis of no herding.

The key to understanding this measure is to note that it indicates that $\Pr_{i,j}(\Theta,T) > \Pr_{i,j}$ if $\Theta > 0$ and $\Pr_{i,j}(\Theta,T) < \Pr_{i,j}$ if $\Theta < 0$. That is, a positive estimate of Θ suggests a tendency to herd whereas a negative estimate suggests a tendency to deviate from the consensus (to antiherd). The idea behind estimating Θ from this arbitrarily specified function is to let the data dictate the probability of no herding; doing so circumvents the problem caused by the lack of theory regarding the underlying distribution if no herding is present.

Depending on the consensus recommendation used (e.g., a simple average of prevailing recommendations or a weighted-average of recommendations with weights based on measures of the quality of the brokerage house making the recommendation), Welch found that the estimate of Θ ranges from 0.13 to 0.16. For Welch's sample of stock recommendations, this range implies that the probability of hitting a target recommendation of hold was 42–47 percent.

The positive values of Θ that Welch found suggest that the prevailing consensus and the two most recent revisions by other analysts influence analysts' stock recommendations, which is consistent with herding in analysts' stock recommendations. Furthermore, Welch found that revisions have a stronger influence on herding behavior if they are recent and if they are good predictors of future security returns. The effect of the prevailing consensus, however, does not depend on whether it is a good predictor of subsequent stock returns. Welch concluded that herding toward recent revisions stems from a desire to exploit short-term information about fundamentals; herding toward the consensus is less likely to be driven by information about fundamentals.

Herding in Analysts' Earnings Forecasts. If individuals herd, they will not make full use of their private information and, therefore, may overrely on public information. This pattern is consistent with prior literature documenting analysts' tendency to misinterpret new information. De Bondt and Thaler (1990) found that consensus earnings forecasts systematically overreact to new information. Overreaction is consistent with herding, but many other papers have provided evidence that analysts *underreact* to new information (e.g., Abarbanell and Bernard 1992), which is inconsistent with herding.

Lamont (2002) used data on forecasts of macroeconomic indicators to test for the effect of the forecaster's reputation on her or his forecasts. Lamont's focus was on the "boldness" of the forecasts, where boldness captures how far the forecast deviates from the consensus. Bolder forecasts deviate more from the consensus forecast (in either direction) than do tentative forecasts. Lamont found that, relative to more junior forecasters, more senior forecasters issued bolder, but not necessarily more accurate, forecasts. He interpreted these results as consistent with a career-concerns-based herding model in which junior analysts have incentives to herd (i.e., issue forecasts that deviate less from the consensus).

Hong et al. provided additional evidence on the career-concerns explanation for analyst herding. They examined a large sample of earnings forecasts from the Institutional Brokers Estimate System (I/B/E/S) for 1983–1996. They found that analysts with poor forecast accuracy are less likely to be promoted and more likely to be fired. Conditional on the inexperienced analysts' forecast accuracy, however, the inexperienced analysts were more likely than their experienced colleagues to suffer career setbacks when they made bold predictions. These results provide some evidence that "going out on a limb" and being wrong when you are inexperienced is costly in career terms. Moreover, bucking the consensus and being right does not significantly add to career prospects. Hong et al. concluded that this pattern of incentives encourages inexperienced analysts to take fewer risks than their experienced counterparts, which is consistent with herding behavior on the part of inexperienced analysts.

A limitation in using the boldness measure (defined as the absolute distance between the forecast and the consensus) as the measure of herding is that boldness does not uniquely capture herding. Rather, the distance between the forecast and the consensus will capture the degree of analysts' herding behavior and the precision of the analysts' private information. In other words, one might observe a tentative forecast (i.e., one close to the consensus) either because the analyst is purposely underutilizing a private signal and herding toward the consensus or because the analyst is receiving a very imprecise signal. Because researchers cannot observe the analyst's signal or its precision, a forecast close to the consensus does not necessarily indicate herding; it may simply mean the existence of an imprecise signal.

Zitzewitz (2001) proposed a measure of herding that overcomes this problem with the boldness measure. His approach focused on the coefficient estimate from regressing the forecast error for the consensus forecast on the deviation between an analyst's forecast and the consensus. In such a regression, a coefficient greater than 1 indicates overweighting and a coefficient less than 1 indicates underweighting. The intuition for this measure is as follows:

If an analyst rationally uses all information in the consensus, any deviation of his forecast from the consensus should be to correct, on average, the forecast errors in the consensus. For example, if the consensus contains $1.00 of errors on average, then a deviation from the consensus by $0.80, which gives rise to a coefficient estimate of 0.80, indicates the analyst is underweighting his own signal (because he should have deviated by an additional $0.20). Similarly, a deviation of $1.20, which gives rise to a coefficient estimate of 1.20, indicates that the analyst is overweighting his own signal (because he should have deviated less by $0.20).

Zitzewitz (2001) found in his sample of I/B/E/S forecasts for 1993–1999 that analysts, on average, overweight. This finding suggests that analysts, if anything, exaggerate rather than herd.

Chen and Jiang (2003) developed two measures of analysts' herding tendencies. They studied whether analysts' weightings of their private and public information deviate from the benchmark efficient weights. They defined efficient weights as the weights on signals that form a rational, Bayesian forecast. Their first measure was the estimate of the slope coefficient, β, from regressing the forecast error, *FE*, in the analyst's forecast on the deviation between this forecast and the consensus forecast at the time the forecast was issued, *DEV*. The idea is that forecast errors should not be predictable from available information if analysts efficiently weight their private and public information signals. Intuitively, a positive (negative) value of β means that the analyst's forecast deviates too much (too little) from the consensus relative to the forecast that minimizes the forecast error. When a forecast deviates too much, the analyst is placing too much weight on private information and too little weight on the consensus; this pattern suggests boldness. In contrast, when a forecast deviates too little, the analyst is placing too little weight on her private information and too much weight on the consensus; this pattern implies herding.

Chen and Jiang's (2003) second measure of herding is based on the sign of the analyst's average forecast error and the sign of the deviation. Specifically, they calculated the percentage of time the sign of *FE* equaled the sign of *DEV*, denoted by π. The intuition for this measure is as follows: If analysts use Bayesian weighting, their forecasts should be correct, on average, and the probability that their forecasts (mistakenly) will deviate too much from the consensus should be equal to the probability that their forecasts will (mistakenly) deviate too little from the consensus. In this case, π should be 50 percent. If analysts overweight their private information, however, their forecasts are more likely to overestimate realized earnings *and* to exceed consensus earnings. Hence, π will exceed 50 percent. If analysts herd and, therefore, underweight their private information, π will be less than 50 percent.

For a sample of more than 1.3 million quarterly earnings forecasts made during 1985–2001, both of Chen and Jiang's (2003) measures showed that, on average, analysts overweight their private information. When the authors partitioned the sample into positive and negative deviations from the consensus (i.e., positive and negative values of *DEV*), they found strong evidence of overweighting only for the positive-deviation subsample. For the negative-deviation subsample, they found that analysts underweight their private information, which is consistent with herding toward the consensus.

Other Evidence of Herding. Evidence in Cooper, Day, and Lewis (2001) suggests that some analysts herd regarding *when* they issue forecasts. For a sample of 6,947 forecasts made during 1993–1995, they found that analysts with little ability were more likely to issue forecasts after observing forecasts made by higher-ability analysts. They measured herding in forecast timing by calculating the ratio of the average number of times an analyst's forecasts followed other forecasts to the average number of times the same analyst's forecasts were followed by other forecasts. If an analyst systematically released forecast revisions before other analysts, this lead-to-follower statistic was greater than 1. Cooper et al. found that, relative to analysts with small lead–follower ratios, analysts with large ratios tend to issue more accurate forecasts and their forecasts generate larger trading volume.

Conclusion

This chapter surveyed the literature on analysts' and fund managers' herding behavior. In addition to introducing the main theories about why individuals herd, we discussed how specific features of security analysts' information environments and incentives may give rise to herding behavior. Although the evidence of herding in stock returns is relatively weak, a significant body of research has documented that security analysts exhibit herding in their stock recommendations and earnings forecasts.

5. Conclusion

The goal of this monograph was to summarize the extant academic research on security analyst independence and, where appropriate, to produce or describe the results of research probing the gaps in or conflicting elements of this literature. Research investigating independence issues is necessarily indirect (that is, the researcher typically cannot observe how potential incentives affect the independence of particular analysts). Hence, conclusions and inferences drawn from this research are necessarily based on indirect tests; for example, they are based on researchers' large-sample analyses of such variables as analyst forecast errors. Given that forecast errors (that is, the scaled difference between actual earnings and forecasted earnings) are themselves affected by choices made by the analyst and the researcher (for example, with respect to what earnings number is being forecasted), we are cautious in drawing strong conclusions from research that does not take these choices into consideration. In particular, Chapter 1 emphasized the importance of loss observations and definitional consistency in forecasted earnings and actual earnings in drawing inferences from properties of the distribution of forecast errors.

Our intent in Chapters 2, 3, and 4 was to expose the reader to the major findings of research examining (Chapter 2) factors that influence analyst bias, including institutional incentives, selection, and cognitive biases; (Chapter 3) research into how the management of client companies may affect properties of analysts' forecasts; and (Chapter 4) research into how analysts influence each other. With appropriate caveats about the limitations of drawing inferences from indirect tests, this body of work generally concludes that analysts' decisions, forecasts, and recommendations are affected by all of these influences, albeit in varying degrees.

Will similar findings be made 10 or 20 years from now if these tests are repeated? Of course, the future is unpredictable, but regulatory changes and trends in the security analyst industry suggest that the findings of future research on security analysts may look very different from the way it has looked.

On this point, note that a number of changes have already occurred that are likely to influence researchers' findings concerning security analyst reports. For example, reforms in the security analyst industry spurred by New York State Attorney General Eliot Spitzer will almost surely affect the perceptions and reality of security analyst independence. In addition to fines paid (approximately $1.4 billion by April 2003), the investment banking firms agreed to prohibitions on analysts receiving compensation for investment banking activities and on analysts being involved in the solicitation of investment banking business. As an additional mechanism for discouraging potential conflicts of interest arising from investment banking revenue, the agreement requires that investment banks stop linking the budgets of their research departments to investment banking revenues. Instead, research budgets may be tied to trading commissions, which are themselves declining in the face of inexpensive Internet-based trading mechanisms available to individual investors.

Davis (2004) noted that the inability to tie research budgets to such fees is likely to result in a reduction in research budgets at many investment banking houses. Such a budget reduction may manifest itself in reduced coverage of companies, outsourcing of research, and/or increased work loads for individual analysts. Some evidence that company coverage has dropped is provided by research from the *Wall Street Journal* (see Davis), which reported data indicating that for seven major investment banking firms, the average number of companies covered in 2003 was 2,126, compared with 2,585 in 2000. Evidence of declining research budgets has been reported by Sanford C. Bernstein and Company, which found that the total research budgets of the eight largest investment banking firms (Merrill Lynch & Company, Credit Suisse First Boston, Smith Barney, JPMorgan Chase, Goldman Sachs, Morgan Stanley, Lehman Brothers, and Bear, Stearns & Company) declined from $2.7 billion in 2000 to $1.7 billion in 2003.

What do these declines in spending and coverage imply about the analyst industry? Davis suggested several possible effects. First, these declines imply a movement, which is already occurring, among large institutions (including mutual funds and hedge funds) away from sell-side analyst research toward boutique research firms that service a significantly smaller client base. The niche filled by these boutique firms (many of which are small and entrepreneurial in nature) is providing deep research on particular issues and questions confronting the large investor; this kind of research is sometimes referred to as "bespoke research." Second, the reduced budgets and increased work demands may render the security analyst industry less attractive than it has been in the past, although U.S. Bureau of Labor Statistics data indicate that securities and commodities industry employment increased from May 2003 to approximately 780,000 individuals in the first quarter of 2004 (but was down from an all-time high of approximately 841,000 in the first quarter of 2001). Added to the concern about the attractiveness of the profession itself are the restrictions and additional administrative burdens imposed on analysts because of reforms that are likely to reduce the amount of time they can devote to equity research. Finally, Regulation Fair Disclosure (Reg FD) has most surely changed the analyst's work environment because the regulation prohibits providing information in one-on-one meetings with analysts that is not also disseminated to the public.

In summary, regulatory changes have almost certainly made the sell-side analyst's job more difficult. Whether such costs are worth the benefits that the changes produce will be determined in the future when we can analyze the effects of these regulatory initiatives.

The trend in the industry appears to be moving away from traditional sell-side research toward more-focused research aimed at (if not commissioned by) small, wealthy investors or funds. Such a shift is a concern because the participation of middle-income individual investors who are small players in the stock market is increasing. A 2002 joint study undertaken by the Investment Company Institute and the Securities Industry Association (ICI/SEI 2002) indicated that 84.3 million individuals in the United States (49.5 percent of U.S. households) owned stock or stock mutual funds at that time (versus 42.4 million individuals and 19 percent of U.S. households in 1983). These numbers are substantial in both the proportion of household assets invested and economywide holdings. U.S. Federal Reserve data for 2003 indicated that 75 percent of Americans' liquid assets were invested in stocks, bonds, and mutual funds (versus 45 percent in 1975) and that the dollar magnitude of these holdings has increased almost tenfold in the past 20 years—from $1.7 trillion dollars in 1975 to $16.5 trillion dollars as of the fourth quarter of 2003. Presumably, many of these investment decisions were informed, in some way, by security analysts' research. Although understandable from a purely economic perspective, if the research industry begins to target wealthier individuals and funds even more aggressively than it has, these small individual investors may be disadvantaged. Such an informational disadvantage runs counter to the goal of recent regulatory actions—in particular, Reg FD.

The trend toward boutique research also increases the interest of researchers in the properties of buy-side analysts' forecasts, which have been largely ignored by researchers because of the limited publicly available data on buy-side forecasts. An exception is Willis (2001), who studied properties of portfolio managers' stock recommendations reported in *Barron's*. We hope that data providers—and buy-side analysts themselves and their employers—will allow the span of coverage by academic research to increase to include the forecasts, recommendations, and price targets of buy-side analysts. Such a data expansion would provide a rich and fertile ground for exploring issues of security analyst independence.

How the trends we see today will affect the next generation of sell-side analysts is also an open question. Certainly, we expect that the next generation will face an institutional setting that is different from the one covered by much of existing research. By the very nature of the regulatory reforms, the effects of institutional incentives on analysts' forecasts should diminish. We also expect to see a wider array of stock recommendations being issued as pressure increases for analysts to report their true beliefs and for investment banks to publicize the distribution of their firms' stock selections. This expansion is likely to increase the scope of analysts' reports, in terms of the financial and nonfinancial elements probed and in the breadth of topics addressed.

As competition for superior research heightens, we also expect that analysts will demand more and better training in financial analysis, valuation methods, and financial reporting. This training need not be limited, as it has in the past, to an emphasis on studying U.S. accounting practices. The Financial Accounting Standards Board, which promulgates accounting rules in the United States, and the International Accounting Standards Board are committed to working toward global convergence in accounting practices.[45] Such a convergence enhances the opportunities for security analysts to engage in worldwide equity research and also mirrors U.S. investor interest in foreign stock ownership, which has increased significantly in the past 20 years. These increased demands create opportunities for educational institutions and for industry groups to design programs tailored to provide the sort of in-depth, industry-specific knowledge that good fundamental analysis requires.

---

[45]In October 2002, the FASB and the IASB issued the Norwalk Agreement, a memorandum of understanding formalizing their commitment to the convergence of U.S. and international accounting standards.

References

Abarbanell, Jeffrey, and Victor Bernard. 1992. "Tests of Analysts' Overreaction/Underreaction to Earnings Information as an Explanation for Anomalous Stock Price Behavior." *Journal of Finance*, vol. 47, no. 3 (July):1181–1207.

Abarbanell, Jeffery, and Reuven Lehavy. 2002. "Differences in Commercial Database Reported Earnings: Implications for Empirical Research." Working paper, University of North Carolina and University of Michigan.

———. 2003. "Biased Forecasts or Biased Earnings? The Role of Reported Earnings in Explaining Apparent Bias and Over/Underreaction in Analysts' Earnings Forecasts." *Journal of Accounting and Economics*, vol. 36, nos. 1–3 (December):105–146.

Affleck-Graves, John, Larry Davis, and Richard Mendenhall. 1990. "Forecasts of Earnings per Share: Possible Sources of Analyst Superiority and Bias." *Contemporary Accounting Research*, vol. 6, no. 2 (Spring):501–517.

Agrawal, Anup, and Sahiba Chadha. 2003. "Who Is Afraid of Reg FD? The Behavior and Performance of Sell-Side Analysts Following the SEC's Fair Disclosure Rules." Working paper, University of Alabama.

AIMR. 2001. "Regulation FD e-Survey Summary." Charlottesville, VA: Association for Investment Management and Research (now, CFA Institute): www.cfainstitute.com/pressroom/01releases/regFD_surveysum.html.

Akerlof, George. 1980. "A Theory of Social Custom, of Which Unemployment May Be One Consequence." *Quarterly Journal of Economics*, vol. 94, no. 4 (June):749–775.

Ali, Ashiq, April Klein, and James Rosenfeld. 1992. "Analysts' Use of Information about Permanent and Transitory Earnings Components in Forecasting Annual EPS." *Accounting Review*, vol. 67, no. 1 (January):183–198.

Asquith, Paul, Michael Mikhail, and Andrea Au. Forthcoming 2004. "Information Content of Equity Analyst Reports." *Journal of Financial Economics*.

Avery, Christopher, and Judith Chevalier. 1999. "Herding over the Career." *Economics Letters,* vol. 63, no. 3 (June):327–333.

Baber, William, and Sok-Hyon Kang. 2002. "The Impact of Split Adjusting and Rounding on Analysts' Forecast Error Calculations." *Accounting Horizons*, vol. 16, no. 4 (December):277–290.

Bailey, Warren, Haitao Li, Connie Mao, and Rui Zhong. 2003. "Regulation Fair Disclosure and Earnings Information: Market, Analyst, and Corporate Responses." *Journal of Finance*, vol. 58, no. 6 (December):2487–2514.

Banerjee, Abhijit. 1992. "A Simple Model of Herd Behavior." *Quarterly Journal of Economics*, vol. 107, no. 3 (August):797–817.

Barron, Orie, Oliver Kim, Steve Lim, and Douglas Stevens. 1998. "Using Analysts' Forecasts to Measure Properties of Analysts' Information Environment." *Accounting Review*, vol. 73, no. 4 (October):421–433.

Barth, Mary, John Elliott, and Mark Finn. 1999. "Market Rewards Associated with Patterns of Increasing Earnings." *Journal of Accounting Research*, vol. 37, no. 2 (Autumn):387–413.

Basu, Sudipta, and Stanimir Markov. 2003. "Loss Function Assumptions in Rational Expectations Tests on Financial Analysts' Earnings Forecasts." Working paper, Emory University.

Begg, Colin, and Robert Gray. 1984. "Calculation of Polychotomous Logistic Regression Parameters Using Individualized Regressions." *Biometrika*, vol. 71, no. 1:11–18.

Bhattacharya, Nilabhra, Ervin Black, Theodore Christensen, and Chad Larson. 2003. "Assessing the Relative Informativeness and Permanence of Pro Forma Earnings and GAAP Operating Earnings." *Journal of Accounting & Economics*, vol. 36, nos. 1–3 (December):285–319.

Bikhachandani, Sushil, and Sunil Sharma. 2001. "Herd Behavior in Financial Markets." *IMF Staff Papers*, vol. 47, no. 3:279–310.

Bikhachandani, Sushil, David Hirshleifer, and Ivo Welch. 1998. "Learning from the Behavior of Others: Conformity, Fads, and Informational Cascades." *Journal of Economic Perspectives*, vol. 12, no. 3 (Summer):151–170.

Bradshaw, Mark, and Richard Sloan. 2002. "GAAP versus the Street: An Empirical Assessment of Two Alternative Definitions of Earnings." *Journal of Accounting Research*, vol. 40, no. 1 (March):41–66.

Brav, Alon. 2000. "Inference in Long-Horizon Event Studies: A Bayesian Approach with Application to Initial Public Offerings." *Journal of Finance*, vol. 55, no. 5 (October):1979–2016.

Brav, Alon, and Paul Gompers. 1997. "Myth or Reality? The Long-Run Underperformance of Initial Public Offerings: Evidence from Venture and Nonventure Capital Backed Companies." *Journal of Finance*, vol. 52, no. 5 (December):1791–1821.

Brav, Alon, Christopher Geczy, and Paul Gompers. 2000. "Is the Abnormal Return Following Equity Issuances Anomalous?" *Journal of Financial Economics*, vol. 56, no. 2 (May):209–249.

Brown, Keith, W.V. Harlow, and Laura Starks. 1996. "Of Tournaments and Temptations: An Analysis of Managerial Incentives in the Mutual Fund Industry." *Journal of Finance*, vol. 51, no. 1 (March):85–110.

Brown, Lawrence. 2001. "A Temporal Analysis of Earnings Surprises: Profits versus Losses." *Journal of Accounting Research*, vol. 39, no. 2 (September):221–241.

Brown, Lawrence, and Kumar Sivakumar. 2001. "Comparing the Quality of Three Earnings Measures." Collected Abstracts of the American Accounting Association's Annual Meeting.

Brown, Lawrence, Gordon Richardson, and Steven Schwager. 1987. "An Information Interpretation of Financial Analyst Superiority in Forecasting Earnings." *Journal of Accounting Research*, vol. 25, no. 1 (Spring):49–67.

Brown, Lawrence, Paul Griffin, Robert Hagerman, and Mark Zmijewski. 1987. "Security Analyst Superiority Relative to Univariate Time-Series Models in Forecasting Quarterly Earnings." *Journal of Accounting and Economics*, vol. 9, no. 1 (April):61–87.

Brown, Paul, George Foster, and Eric Noreen. 1985. *Security Analyst Multi-Year Earnings Forecasts and the Capital Market*. Studies in Accounting Research, Monograph No. 21, Sarasota, FL: American Accounting Association.

Brown, Stephen, Stephen Hillegeist, and Kin Lo. 2002. "Voluntary Disclosure Frequency and Information Asymmetry." Working paper, Emory University, Northwestern University, and University of British Columbia.

Bushee, Brian, Dawn Matsumoto, and Gregory Miller. 2002. "Managerial and Investor Responses to Disclosure Regulation: The Case of Reg FD and Conference Calls." Working paper, University of Pennsylvania, University of Washington, and Harvard University.

"Canadian Regulator Clarifies Disclosure Rules." 2002. *Investor Relations Business* (20 May):1.

Chen, Qi, and Wei Jiang. 2003. "Analysts' Weighting of Public and Private Information." Working paper, Duke University and Columbia University.

———. 2004. "The Role of Forecast Patterns in Conveying Analysts' Predictive Ability." Working paper, Duke University and Columbia University.

Chevalier, Judith, and Glenn Ellison. 1997. "Risk Taking by Mutual Funds as a Response to Incentives." *Journal of Political Economy*, vol. 105, no. 6 (December):1167–1200.

———. 1999. "Career Concerns of Mutual Fund Managers." *Quarterly Journal of Economics*, vol. 114, no. 2 (May):389–432.

Choe, Hyuk, Bong-Chan Kho, and Rene Stultz. 1999. "Do Foreign Investors Destabilize Stock Markets? The Korean Experience in 1997." *Journal of Financial Economics*, vol. 54, no. 2 (October):227–264.

Christie, William, and Roger Huang. 1995. "Following the Pied Piper: Do Individual Returns Herd around the Market?" *Financial Analysts Journal*, vol. 51, no. 4 (July/August):31–37.

Cianci, Anna. 2000. "Motivational and Cognitive Sources of Financial Analysts' Overoptimistic Earnings Forecasts." Working paper, University of Florida.

Clement, Michael. 1999. "Analyst Forecast Accuracy: Do Ability, Resources, and Portfolio Complexity Matter?" *Journal of Accounting and Economics*, vol. 27, no. 3 (June):285–303.

Cohen, Daniel, and Thomas Lys. 2003. "A Note on Analysts' Earnings Forecast Errors Distribution." *Journal of Accounting and Economics,* vol. 36, nos. 1–3 (December):147–164.

Collins, Daniel, Edward Maydew, and Ira Weiss. 1997. "Changes in the Value-Relevance of Earnings and Book Values over the Past Forty Years." *Journal of Accounting and Economics*, vol. 24, no. 1 (December):39–68.

Cooper, Rick A., Theodore E. Day, and Craig M. Lewis. 2001. "Following the Leader: A Study of Individual Analysts' Earnings Forecasts." *Journal of Financial Economics*, vol. 61, no. 3 (September):383–416.

Cotter, Julie, Irem Tuna, and Peter Wysocki. Forthcoming 2004. "Expectation Management and Beatable Targets: How Do Analysts React to Explicit Earnings Guidance?" *Contemporary Accounting Research*.

Daniel, Kent, David Hirshleifer, and Siew Hong Teoh. 2002. "Investor Psychology in Capital Markets: Evidence and Policy Implications." *Journal of Monetary Economics*, vol. 49, no. 1 (January):139–209.

Das, Samnath, Carolyn Levine, and K. Sivaramakrishnan. 1998. "Earnings Predictability and Bias in Analysts' Earnings Forecasts." *Accounting Review*, vol. 73, no. 2 (April):285–302.

Davis, Ann. 2004. "Increasingly, Stock Research Serves the Pros, Not 'Little Guy'—In the Wake of Spitzer Pact, Wall Street and Upstarts Are Catering to Elite Few—Ordering 'Bespoke' Reports." *Wall Street Journal* (5 March):A1.

De Bondt, Werner, and Richard H. Thaler. 1990. "Do Security Analysts Overreact?" *American Economic Review Papers and Proceedings*, vol. 80, no. 2 (May):52–57.

Dechow, Patricia, Amy Hutton, and Richard Sloan. 2000. "The Relation between Analysts' Forecasts of Long-Term Earnings Growth and Stock Price Performance Following Equity Offerings." *Contemporary Accounting Research*, vol. 17, no. 1 (Spring):1–32.

Degeorge, François, Jayendu Patel, and Richard Zeckhauser. 1999. "Earnings Management to Exceed Thresholds." *Journal of Business*, vol. 72, no 1 (January):1–33.

Devenow, Andrea, and Ivo Welch. 1996. "Rational Herding in Financial Economics." *European Economic Review*, vol. 40, nos. 3–5 (April):603–615.

Dewatripont, Mathias, Ian Jewitt, and Jean Tirole. 1999. "The Economics of Career Concerns, Part II: Application to Missions and Accountability of Government Agencies." *Review of Economic Studies*, vol. 66, no. 1 (January):199–217.

Diamond, Douglas, and Philip Dybvig. 1983. "Bank Runs, Deposit Insurance, and Liquidity." *Journal of Political Economy*, vol. 91, no. 3 (June):401–419.

Dorfman, John. 1991. "Heard on the Street: Analysts Devote More Time to Selling as Firms Keep Scorecard on Performance." *Wall Street Journal* (29 October):C1.

Dowen, Richard. 1996. "Analyst Reaction to Negative Earnings for Large Well-Known Firms." *Journal of Portfolio Management*, vol. 23, no. 1 (Fall):49–55.

Dugar, Amitabh, and Siva Nathan. 1995. "The Effects of Investment Banking Relationships on Financial Analysts' Earnings Forecasts and Investment Recommendations." *Contemporary Accounting Research*, vol. 12, no. 1 (Fall):131–160.

Eames, Michael, Steven Glover, and Jane Kennedy. 2002. "The Association between Trading Recommendations and Broker-Analysts' Earnings Forecasts." *Journal of Accounting Research*, vol. 40, no. 1 (March):85–104.

Easley, David, Nicholas Kiefer, and Maureen O'Hara. 1997. "One Day in the Life of a Very Common Stock." *Review of Financial Studies*, vol. 10, no. 3 (Autumn):805–835.

Easterwood, John, and Stacey Nutt. 1999. "Inefficiency in Analysts' Earnings Forecasts: Systematic Misreaction or Systematic Optimism?" *Journal of Finance*, vol. 54, no. 5 (October):1777–97.

Eccles, Robert, and Dwight Crane. 1988. *Doing Deals: Investment Banks at Work*. Boston, MA: Harvard Business School Press.

Ehrbeck, Tilman, and Robert Waldmann. 1996. "Why Are Professional Forecasters Biased? Agency versus Behavioral Explanations." *Quarterly Journal of Economics*, vol. 111, no. 1 (February):21–41.

Eleswarapu, Venkat, Rex Thompson, and Kumar Venkataraman. 2004. "Measuring the Fairness of Regulation Fair Disclosure through Its Impact on Trading Costs and Information Asymmetry." *Journal of Financial and Quantitative Analysis*, vol. 39, no. 2 (June):209–225.

Elliott, John, and J. Douglas Hanna. 1996. "Repeated Accounting Write-Offs and the Information Content of Earnings." *Journal of Accounting Research*, vol. 34 (Supplement):135–155.

Elton, Edwin, Martin Gruber, and Seth Grossman. 1986. "Discrete Expectational Data and Portfolio Performance." *Journal of Finance*, vol. 41, no. 3 (July):699–713.

FAJ. 1999. Behavioral Finance issue of the *Financial Analysts Journal*, vol. 55, no. 6 (November/December).

Fama, Eugene. 1980. "Agency Problems and the Theory of the Firm." *Journal of Political Economy*, vol. 88, no. 2 (April):288–307.

Fama, Eugene, and Kenneth French. 1993. "Common Risk Factors in the Returns on Stocks and Bonds." *Journal of Financial Economics*, vol. 33, no. 1 (February):3–56.

FERF. *Investor Information Needs and the Annual Report*. 1987. Florham Park, NJ: Financial Executives Research Foundation.

Francis, Jennifer, and Donna R. Philbrick. 1993. "Analysts' Decisions as Products of a Multi-Task Environment." *Journal of Accounting Research*, vol. 31, no. 2 (Autumn):216–230.

Francis, Jennifer, and Leonard Soffer. 1997. "The Relative Informativeness of Analysts' Stock Recommendations and Earnings Forecast Revisions." *Journal of Accounting Research*, vol. 35, no. 2 (Autumn):193–211.

Francis, Jennifer, Dhananjay Nanda, and Xin Wang. 2004. "Re-examining the Effects of Regulation Fair Disclosure Using Foreign Listed Firms to Control for Concurrent Shocks." Working paper, Duke University.

Francis, Jennifer, Katherine Schipper, and Linda Vincent. 2002. "Earnings Announcements and Competing Information." *Journal of Accounting and Economics*, vol. 33, no. 3 (August):313–342.

Fried, Dov, and Daniel Givoly. 1982. "Financial Analysts' Forecasts of Earnings: A Better Surrogate for Market Expectations." *Journal of Accounting and Economics*, vol. 4, no. 2 (October):85–107.

Friend, Irwin, Marshall Blume, and Jean Crockett. 1970. *Mutual Funds and Other Institutional Investors: A New Perspective.* New York, NY: McGraw-Hill.

Gadarowski, Christopher, and Praveen Sinha. 2002. "On the Efficacy of Regulation Fair Disclosure: Theory and Evidence." Working paper, Cornell University.

Gintschel, Andreas, and Stanimir Markov. 2003. "The Effectiveness of Regulation FD." Working paper, Deutsche Bank and Emory University.

Givoly, Daniel, and Josef Lakonishok. 1979. "The Information Content of Financial Analysts' Forecasts of Earnings: Some Evidence on Semi-Strong Inefficiency" *Journal of Accounting and Economics*, vol. 1, no. 3 (December):165–185.

Graham, John. 1999. "Herding among Investment Newsletters: Theory and Evidence." *Journal of Finance*, vol. 54, no. 1 (February):237–268.

Grasso, Richard A. 2003. Summary of the Statement of Richard A. Grasso, Chairman and CEO of the New York Stock Exchange, Inc. to the United States Senate Committee on Banking, Housing and Urban Affairs (7 May): banking.senate.gov/03_05hrg/050703/grasso.pdf.

Grinblatt, Mark, Sheridan Titman, and Russell Wermers. 1995. "Momentum Investment Strategies, Portfolio Performance, and Herding: A Study of Mutual Fund Behavior." *American Economic Review*, vol. 85, no. 5 (December):1088–1105.

Gu, Zhaoyang, and Ting Chen. 2003. "In or Out: Do Analysts Know What They Are Doing with Nonrecurring Items?" Working paper, Carnegie Mellon University.

Hansen, Robert, and Atulya Sarin. 1998. "Are Analysts Overoptimistic around Seasoned Equity Offerings?" Working paper, Virginia Tech and Santa Clara University.

Hayes, Rachel. 1998. "The Impact of Trading Commission Incentives on Analysts' Stock Coverage Decisions and Earnings Forecasts." *Journal of Accounting Research*, vol. 36, no. 2 (Autumn):299–320.

Hayes, Rachel, and Carolyn Levine. 2000. "An Approach to Adjusting Analysts' Consensus Forecasts for Selection Bias." *Contemporary Accounting Research*, vol. 17, no. 1 (Spring):61–83.

Heflin, Frank, K.R. Subramanyam, and Yuan Zhang. 2003a. "Regulation FD and the Financial Information Environment: Early Evidence." *Accounting Review*, vol. 78, no. 1 (January):1–37.

———. 2003b. "Stock Return Volatility Before and After Regulation FD." Working paper, Purdue University, University of Southern California, and Columbia University.

Hirshleifer, David, and Siew Hong Teoh. 2003. "Herd Behavior and Cascading in Capital Markets: A Review and Synthesis." *European Financial Management*, vol. 9, no. 1 (March): 25–66.

Holmstrom, Bengt. 1999. "Managerial Incentive Problems: A Dynamic Perspective." *Review of Economic Studies*, vol. 66, no. 1 (January):169–182.

Hong, Harrison, and Jeffrey Kubik. 2003. "Analyzing the Analysts: Career Concerns and Biased Earnings Forecasts." *Journal of Finance*, vol. 58, no. 1 (February):313–351.

Hong, Harrison, Jeffrey Kubik, and Amit Solomon. 2000. "Security Analysts' Career Concerns and Herding of Earnings Forecasts." *Rand Journal of Economics*, vol. 31, no. 1 (Spring):121–144.

Huang, Allen, Richard Willis, and Amy Zang. 2004. "Bold Security Analysts' Forecasts and Managers' Information Flow." Working paper, Duke University.

Hwang, Lee Seok, Ching-Lih Jan, and Sudipta Basu. 1996. "Loss Firms and Analysts' Earnings Forecast Errors." *Journal of Financial Statement Analysis*, vol. 1, no. 2 (Winter):18–30.

I/B/E/S. 2001. Monthly Comments (February): www.ntu.edu.sg/lib/collections/db/ABB-8140.htm.

ICI/SEI. 2002. "Equity Ownership in America." Washington, DC: Investment Company Institute and Securities Industry Association: www.ici.org/shareholders/dec/1rpt_02_equity_owners.pdf.

Irani, Afshad, and Irene Karamanou. 2003. "Regulation Fair Disclosure, Analyst Following, and Analyst Forecast Dispersion." *Accounting Horizons*, vol. 17, no. 1 (March):15–29.

Irvine, Paul. 2000. "Do Analysts Generate Trade for Their Firms? Evidence from the Toronto Stock Exchange." *Journal of Accounting and Economics*, vol. 30, no. 2 (October):209–226.

Jacob, John, and Thomas Lys. 1999. "Determinants and Implications of the Auto-Correlation in Analysts' Forecast Errors." Working paper, University of Colorado and Northwestern University.

Jacob, John, Thomas Lys, and Margaret Neale. 1999. "Expertise in Forecasting Performance of Security Analysts." *Journal of Accounting and Economics*, vol. 28, no. 1 (November):51–82.

Janvrin, Diane, and Jim Kurtenbach. 2002. "The Impact of Regulation Fair Disclosure on the Information Environment: Evidence from Providers and Users." Working paper, Iowa State University.

Kasznik, Ronald, and Maureen McNichols. 2002. "Does Meeting Earnings Expectations Matter? Evidence from Analyst Forecast Revisions and Share Prices." *Journal of Accounting Research*, vol. 40, no. 3 (June):727–759.

Keane, Michael, and David Runkle. 1998. "Are Financial Analysts' Forecasts of Corporate Profits Rational?" *Journal of Political Economy*, vol. 106, no. 4 (August):768–805.

Keynes, John Maynard. 1936. *The General Theory of Employment, Interest, and Money*. New York, NY: Harcourt Brace.

Kim, Woochan, and Shang-Jin Wei. 1999. "Offshore Investment Funds: Monsters in Emerging Markets." NBER Working Paper No. w7133.

Klein, April. 1990. "A Direct Test of the Cognitive Bias Theory of Share Price Reversals." *Journal of Accounting and Economics*, vol. 13, no. 2 (July):155–166.

Kraus, Alan, and Hans Stoll. 1972. "Parallel Trading by Institutional Investors." *Journal of Financial and Quantitative Analysis*, vol. 7, no. 5 (December):2107–38.

Laderman, Jeffrey. 1998. "Wall Street's Spin Game: Stock Analysts Often Have a Hidden Agenda." *BusinessWeek Online* (5 October).

Lakonishok, Josef, Andrei Shleifer, and Robert Vishny. 1992. "The Impact of Institutional Trading on Stock Prices." *Journal of Financial Economics*, vol. 32, no. 1 (August):23–43.

Lamont, Owen. 2002. "Macroeconomic Forecasts and Microeconomic Forecasters." *Journal of Economic Behavior & Organization*, vol. 48, no. 3 (July):265–280.

Liaw, K. Thomas. 1999. *The Business of Investment Banking*. New York, NY: John Wiley and Sons.

Lim, Terence. 2001. "Rationality and Analysts' Forecast Bias." *Journal of Finance*, vol. 56, no. 1 (February):369–385.

Lin, Hsiou-wei, and Maureen McNichols. 1998. "Underwriting Relationships, Analysts' Earnings Forecasts, and Investment Recommendations." *Journal of Accounting and Economics*, vol. 25, no. 1 (February):101–127.

Lohse, Deborah. 1998. "Tricks of the Trade: 'Buffett Is Buying This' and Other Sayings of the Cold-Call Crew." *Wall Street Journal* (1 June): A1.

Loughran, Tim, and Jay Ritter. 1995. "The New Issues Puzzle." *Journal of Finance*, vol. 50, no. 1 (March):23–51.

Lys, Thomas, and Sungkyu Sohn. 1990. "The Association between Revisions of Financial Analysts' Earnings Forecasts and Security-Price Changes." *Journal of Accounting and Economics*, vol. 13, no. 4 (December):341–363.

Mac, Chi. 2002. "The Effects of Regulation Fair Disclosure on Information Leakage." Working paper, Columbia University.

Matsumoto, Dawn. 2002. "Management's Incentives to Avoid Negative Earnings Surprises." *Accounting Review*, vol. 77, no. 3 (July):483–514.

McNichols, Maureen, and Patricia C. O'Brien. 1997. "Self-Selection and Analyst Coverage." *Journal of Accounting Research*, vol. 35 (Supplement):167–199.

Mendenhall, Richard. 1991. "Evidence on the Possible Underweighting of Earnings-Related Information." *Journal of Accounting Research*, vol. 29, no. 1 (Spring):170–179.

Michaely, Roni, and Kent Womack. 1999. "Conflict of Interest and the Credibility of Underwriter Analyst Recommendations." *Review of Financial Studies*, vol. 12, no. 4 (Special):653–686.

Mikhail, Michael, Beverly Walther, and Richard Willis. 1997. "Do Security Analysts Improve Their Performance with Experience?" *Journal of Accounting Research*, vol. 35, no. 1 (Spring):131–157.

————. 1999. "Does Forecast Accuracy Matter to Security Analysts?" *Accounting Review*, vol. 74, no. 2 (April):185–200.

————. 2003a. "Security Analyst Experience and Post-Earnings-Announcement Drift." *Journal of Accounting, Auditing, and Finance*, vol. 18, no. 4 (Fall):529–550.

————. 2003b. "The Effect of Experience on Security Analyst Underreaction." *Journal of Accounting and Economics*, vol. 35, no. 1 (April):101–116.

Milbourn, Todd, Richard Shockley, and Anjan Thakor. 2001. "Managerial Career Concerns and Investments in Information." *Rand Journal of Economics*, vol. 32, no. 2 (Summer):334–351.

Mohanram, Partha, and Shyam Sunder. 2001 "Has Regulation Fair Disclosure Affected Financial Analysts' Ability to Forecast Earnings?" Working paper, Columbia University and Northwestern University.

Nofsinger, John R., and Richard W. Sias. 1999. "Herding and Feedback Trading by Institutional and Individual Investors." *Journal of Finance,* vol. 54, no. 6 (December):2263–95.

O'Brien, Patricia. 1988. "Analysts' Forecasts as Earnings Expectations." *Journal of Accounting and Economics*, vol. 10, no. 1 (January):53–88.

O'Brien, T.L., and Matt Murray. 1995. "Buffett Boosts American Express Stake to 9.8%, Acquires 8.3% of PNC Bank." *Wall Street Journal* (15 February):A1.

Payne, Jeff, and Wayne Thomas. 2002. "The Implications of Using Stock-Split Adjusted I/B/E/S Data in Empirical Research." Working paper, University of Oklahoma.

Philbrick, Donna, and William Ricks. 1991. "Using Value Line and I/B/E/S Analyst Forecasts in Accounting Research." *Journal of Accounting Research*, vol. 29, no. 2 (Autumn):397–417.

Prendergast, Canice, and Lars Stole. 1996. "Impetuous Youngsters and Jaded Old-Timers: Acquiring a Reputation for Learning." *Journal of Political Economy*, vol. 104, no. 6 (December):1105–34.

Richardson, Scott, Siew Hong Teoh, and Peter Wysocki. Forthcoming 2004. "The Walkdown to Beatable Analyst Forecasts: The Roles of Equity Issuance and Insider Trading Incentives." *Contemporary Accounting Research*.

Scharfstein, David S., and Jeremy C Stein. 1990. "Herd Behavior and Investment." *American Economic Review*, vol. 80, no. 3 (June):465–479.

Shane, Philip, Naomi Soderstrom, and Sung Wook Yoon. 2001. "Earnings and Price Discovery in the Post-Reg. FD Information Environment: A Preliminary Analysis." Working paper, University of Colorado at Boulder.

Shefrin, Hersh. 1999. *Beyond Greed and Fear: Understanding Behavioral Finance and the Psychology of Investing.* Boston, MA: Harvard Business School Publishing.

SIA. 2001. *Costs and Benefits of Regulation Fair Disclosure.* New York, NY: Securities Industry Association.

Siconolfi, Michael. 1995. "'Incredible 'Buys': Many Companies Press Analysts to Steer Clear of Negative Ratings—Stock Research Is Tainted as Naysayers are Banned, Undermined, and Berated—Small Investors in the Dark." *Wall Street Journal* (19 July):A1.

Silverfinger, Warren. 1998. "Finance and Economics." *Economist,* vol. 346, no. 8054 (7 February):76.

Skantz, Terrance, and Barbara Pierce. 2000. "Analyst Forecasts and Analyst Actuals in the Presence of Nonrecurring Gains and Losses: Evidence of Inconsistency." *Advances in Accounting,* vol. 17:221–244.

Solomon, Deborah, and Robert Frank. 2003. "Stock Analysis: You Don't Like Our Stock? You Are Off the List—SEC Sets New Front on Conflicts by Taking Aim at Companies That Retaliate Against Analysts." *Wall Street Journal* (19 June):C1.

Spiess, Katherine, and John Affleck-Graves. 1995. "Underperformance in Long-Run Stock Returns Following Seasoned Equity Offerings." *Journal of Financial Economics,* vol. 38, no. 3 (July):243–267.

Stickel, Scott. 1989. "The Timing of and Incentives for Annual Earnings Forecasts near Interim Earnings Announcements." *Journal of Accounting and Economics,* vol. 11, nos. 2–3 (July):275–292.

———. 1992. "Reputation and Performance among Security Analysts." *Journal of Finance,* vol. 47, no. 5 (December):1811–36.

Straser, Vesa. 2002. "Regulation Fair Disclosure and Information Asymmetry." Working paper, University of Notre Dame.

Sunder, Shyam. 2002. "Investor Access to Conference Call Disclosures: Impact of Regulation Fair Disclosure on Information Asymmetry." Working paper, Northwestern University.

Topaloglu, Selim. 2002. "An Examination of Institutional Trading Activity before and after Regulation FD." Working paper, Purdue University.

Trueman, Brett. 1994. "Analyst Forecasts and Herding Behavior." *Review of Financial Studies*, vol. 7, no. 1 (January):97–124.

Tversky, Amos, and Daniel Kahneman. 1974. "Judgment under Uncertainty: Heuristics and Biases." *Science*, vol. 185:1124–31.

Welch, Ivo. 2000. "Herding among Security Analysts." *Journal of Financial Economics*, vol. 58, no. 3 (December):369–396.

Wermers, Russell. 1999. "Mutual Fund Herding and the Impact on Stock Prices." *Journal of Finance*, vol. 54, no. 2 (April):581–622.

Willis, Richard. 2001. "Mutual Fund Manager Forecasting Behavior." *Journal of Accounting Research*, vol. 39, no. 3 (December):707–725.

Womack, Kent. 1996. "Do Brokerage Analysts' Recommendations Have Investment Value?" *Journal of Finance*, vol. 51, no. 1 (March):137–167.

Zacks History Files. 1999. Zacks Investment Research: zrs.zacks.com/.

Zitzewitz, Eric. 2001. "Measuring Herding and Exaggeration by Equity Analysts and Other Opinion Sellers." Working paper, Stanford University.

———. 2002. "Regulation Fair Disclosure and the Private Information of Analysts." Working paper, Stanford University.